THE COVENANT OF SALT

&

Preservation of the Words of God

Have We Been Untrue To Salt?

H. D. Williams, M. D., Ph. D.

REL067030: Religion: Christian Theology – Apologetics.

ISBN 978-0-9822230-7-9

All Scripture quotes are from the King James Bible except those verses compared and then the source is identified.

Address All Inquiries To:
THE OLD PATHS PUBLICATIONS, Inc.
142 Gold Flume Way
Cleveland, Georgia, U.S.A. 30528

Web: www.theoldpathspublications.com
E-mail: TOP@theoldpathspublications.com

BIBLE FOR TODAY # 3466
Web: www.biblefortoday.org
E-mail: bft@biblefortoday.org

1.0

DEDICATION

This work is dedicated to my precious wife and faithful help meet, Patricia. May God bless each wife who stands with her husband in this battle for *"the salt of the covenant of thy God."*

TABLE OF CONTENTS

TITLE   **PAGE**

"A promise is never better or worse than the character of the one who makes it." (A. W. Tozer)

PREFACE

Preliminaries

This work was written from the author's study notes on salt in the Scripture. It was compiled over a number of years. Hopefully, it will help clarify what many have considered difficult to understand passages, such as Mark 9:49-50 (q.v.). The necessity of salt for physical life parallels the spiritual meaning of salt throughout the Bible. The full understanding of our spiritual need helps us to determine the consistent application of salt all the way through the Scripture. This is no different than the application of the typology of leaven as sin in passages from the Old Testament to the New Testament.

Almost everyone has heard of "rock salt" because it is used in making homemade ice cream. Some will know that NaCl is the atomic structure of salt. When it crystallizes, it forms a rock in the shape of small blocks or cubes (see the picture on the cover). The 'rocks' stuck together form the granules of salt. The Lord Jesus Christ is our Rock.

> Deuteronomy 32:4 "He is the Rock, his work is perfect: for all his ways are judgment: a God of truth and without iniquity, just and right is he."
> 2 Samuel 22:32 For who is God, save the LORD? and who is a rock, save our God?
> 2 Samuel 22:47 The LORD liveth; and blessed be my rock; and exalted be the God of the rock of my salvation.

If this author may be allowed liberty until this work is read and understood, Jesus is our "Rock" of Salt as we shall see. May those who claim His name stand upon the "Rock" and upon His "Salt."

Let the Scripture Speak

In this work, certain words and concepts are repeated often and in different ways to accentuate and clarify them. This is necessary because mind-set all too often prevents us from seeing truth. We must let the Words of God speak and not restricted by previous ideas or thoughts.[1]

The last chapter of this work is an examination of the thoughts and comments by prominent church elders and authors throughout the church age concerning the use of salt in various passages. Some readers may prefer to start there and return to the beginning later. However, many of the considerations by previous authors are wrong. Do not let their reflections hinder your objectivity.

A Recent Plethora of Booklets on Salt

Since 2004, a plethora of booklets on the covenant of salt have appeared on the internet. Some of these may be in response to a message by this author at an Annual Meeting of the Dean Burgon Society in 2004. It appears that many of the booklets continue to make several common errors, which are consistency in application, use of corrupt modern versions, and a denial of the preservation of the Words of God in the Hebrew, Aramaic and Greek Texts underlying the King James Bible.

This Author is Not "King James Only"

This author is not a "King James Only" advocate after the likes of Peter Ruckman or Gail Riplinger. However, he does believe that the King James Bible is the most accurately and faithfully translated

---

[1] The proper way to study the Bible is inductively rather than deductively. We should not bring our ideas to the Bible, but let the Bible form our doctrines, thoughts, and way of life.

English Bible.[2] So, he uses only the King James Bible. He personally believes that every Word of Scripture is important, the word order is often critical, and the underlying proper text in Hebrew, Aramaic, and Greek is the *sine qua non* for translators of the Bible.[3] The importance of this will be understood as the reader progresses through this discussion of salt in the Bible and its relation to preservation of the Words of God.

It is hoped that this work will help the saints of God to appreciate the typology associated with the use of "salt" by our Great God and Saviour, the Lord Jesus Christ (Tit. 2:13).

The time invested in this effort was rewarding to the author beyond measure. It is with great reverence for the Words of God that this author submits this work to His perfect judgment.

---

[2] This author agrees completely with Pastor D. A. Waite, Th.D., Ph.D.'s book, *Defending the King James Bible*. It is available from www.BibleForToday.org.

[3] The author believes that the preserved Words of God in Hebrew, Aramaic, and Greek are the Hebrew Masoretic (2nd Rabbinical ben Chayyim) and Textus Receptus/Traditional Texts underlying the King James Bible. Those texts are the virtually identical Words found in the manuscripts from the days of the apostles and prophets. There are manuscripts promoted by modernistic textual critics that have been demonstrated to be defaced, often changed, and altered to coincide with of the doctrinal beliefs of Gnostics. Those texts are generally called the UBS[4] or Nestle Aland[27] Greek texts and the Hebrew texts (or translations) utilized are the Aleppo, Stuttgart, Samaritan Pentateuch, and Greek Septuagint (LXX) translation of the Old Testament.

"But the axiom in question labours under the far graver defect of disparaging the Divine method, under which in the multitude of evidence preserved all down the ages provision has been made as matter of hard fact, not by weight but by number, for the integrity of the Deposit." (Dean John William Burgon, *The Traditional Text of the Holy Gospels,* p. 44)

CHAPTER 1

WHAT IS A COVENANT?

Some Dictionary Definitions

Several dictionaries define a covenant in the following ways:

"n.
1. A binding agreement; a compact. See Synonyms at bargain.
2. Law
a. A formal sealed agreement or contract.
b. A suit to recover damages for violation of such a contract.
3. In the Bible, God's promise to the human race.
v. **cov·e·nant·ed**, **cov·e·nant·ing**, **cov·e·nants**
v.tr.
To promise by or as if by a covenant.
v.intr.
To enter into a covenant.
[Middle English, from Old French, from present participle of convenir, to agree; see **convene**.]"[4]

Please note definition number three in the quote above. *Collins English Dictionary* defines covenant as the following:

"n
1. a binding agreement; contract
2. (Law) Law
a. an agreement in writing under seal, as to pay a stated annual sum to a charity
b. a particular clause in such an agreement, esp in a

[4] *The American Heritage® Dictionary of the English Language* (Fourth Edition copyright ©2000 by Houghton Mifflin Company. Updated in 2009,. Published by Houghton Mifflin Company. All rights reserved).

lease
3. (Law) (in early English law) an action in which damages were sought for breach of a sealed agreement
4. (Christian Religious Writings / Theology) Bible God's promise to the Israelites and their commitment to worship him alone
vb
(Law) to agree to a covenant (concerning)
[from Old French, from covenir to agree, from Latin convenīre to come together, make an agreement; see CONVENE]
Covenantal...adj
covenantally adv"[5]

Collins English Dictionary also lists the following synonyms:

"noun
1. promise, contract, agreement, commitment, arrangement, treaty, pledge, bargain, convention, pact, compact, concordat, trust *the United Nations covenant on civil and political rights*
2. (Law) deed, contract, bond *If you make regular gifts through a covenant we can reclaim the income tax.*
verb
promise, agree, contract, pledge, bargain, undertake, engage *In the deed of separation, he covenanted that he would not revoke his will.*"[6]

Therefore, a modern contract or covenant has legal components, parts, stipulations, promises, statutes, tenets, conditions, contingencies, agreements, conventions, declarations, or intentions of the implied promise. As some books of law use these terms interchangeably, for the purposes of this work, a contract and a covenant will be considered the same.

---

[5] Collins English Dictionary – Complete and Unabridged 6th Edition 2003. © William Collins Sons & Co. Ltd 1979, 1986 © Harper Collins Publishers 1991, 1994, 1998, 2000, 2003.
[6] Ibid. From http://www.thefreedictionary.com/covenant, accessed on 2/18/2010.

Two Parties Involved

There are always at least two parties involved in a covenant. A Biblical covenant is similar. A Biblical covenant (Hebrew, beriyth; Greek, diatheke) may be conditional or unconditional. If it is conditional, then God expects the appropriate response from man. A conditional covenant is known as an if-then covenant. If man does as God commands, then he will receive the blessings of God. (e.g. Deut. 11:26-28, 28:1ff). If God's covenant is unconditional, God becomes the executor of His contract and He will perform the contract, no matter what man does. An unconditional covenant is known as an "I will" covenant. Examples of unconditional covenants are the Abrahamic (Gen. 12:1-3), Davidic (2 Sam. 7:11-16), Palestinian (Deut. 30:1-10), and New Covenant (Jer. 31). God "will" bring about the specifics in the covenants.

The Bible is a Detailed Covenant

What most students of God's Words fail to appropriate is that the written revelation, which is the sixty-six books of the canon of Scripture, is actually a Covenant (capital "C") between God and man. Most do not link the meaning of Old "Testament" and New "Testament" to the word, "Covenant." Strong's Concordance gives the definition of the underlying Greek word, diatheke (1242), as:

> "properly, a disposition, i.e. (specifically), a contract (especially a divisory will): covenant, testament."

As mentioned above, a contract or covenant constructed by man is a very carefully worded document with expectations and potentials delineated by both parties. Without a doubt, all the Words of God are a very carefully constructed Covenant between God and man.

If we are not certain that the words in a legal contract have not been altered and they are preserved as written, then we can have no confidence in the covenant or contract. God carefully laid out His Words and watches over them as they were copied and transmitted from one generation to another:

> Psalms 105:8 "He hath remembered **his covenant** for ever, **the word** which he commanded to a thousand generations." (cf. Psa. 12:6-7, 33:11, 100:5, 135:13, Mat. 5:17-18, Col. 1:26, 1 Pe. 1:23-25).

When an individual accepts God's gift of salvation by faith (Eph. 2:8-9), he is also accepting God's Covenant with man, which is carefully laid out. This is a spiritual acceptance that is reliant on the Words being preserved. We will discuss how we know that the Words of God are preserved later in this work. Isn't it interesting that "salt" is a 'preservative'?

God's Covenant is detailed to the *"jot and tittle,"* the smallest parts of Hebrew letters, and **preserved** throughout the generations. God said He would do this and He has. The evidence is powerful. Why? Because God wants man to be certain of the Words of His Contract so that there will be no question as to what the Covenant says (Mat. 5:17-18, 24:25, Psa. 12:6-7).

When an individual is converted (born again) (John 3:7), he is reconciled to God (John 3:7, 2 Cor. 5:17-22). He is expected to study God's Covenant, to come under its authority, and to obey the stipulations in it (2 Tim. 2:15, Heb. 5:9). Therefore the document, the sixty-six books, is constructed in such a way that man can live his life as expected by God and revealed in His Words. God's Words express an extensive, detailed Covenant, which gives details in order for man to achieve a sanctified, holy, or 'set aside' life. Following are two very clear aspects of this Covenant:

Presuppositions Are Necessary

1. Man must approach God's Words with certain *a priori* presuppositions as he does for many things in life.[7] They are:
   a. The Covenant is complete for all that pertains to life.
   b. The original Words in the Covenant, which is called Scripture (from the Greek graphé, meaning written Words), in Hebrew, Aramaic, and Greek are perfect and pure (Psa. 12:6-7, Pro. 30:5-6). In modern times, we use two words to emphasize these concepts. Theologians say the words are inerrant and infallible. Inerrant means there are no errors and infallible means the Words are *incapable* of error because they came directly from a perfect, pure, and holy God.
   c. The original Words in Hebrew, Aramaic, and Greek were God-breathed (2 Tim. 3:16). That is, they are not man's words, but Words received from God Himself (Jn. 16:13, 17:8, 14).
   d. The original Words in Hebrew, Aramaic, and Greek are preserved as God promised in His Covenant with man (Psa. 12:6-7, 1 Pet. 1:22-25, Mat. 4:4, 24:35, and many, many other places). The evidence for preservation is overpowering and undeniable.
2. The Words were recorded in heaven before they were ever given to the prophets and apostles to record on manuscripts (hand-written documents) (Psa. 119:89, Dan. 10:21).

The Bible is a Pre-constructed Text

The Covenant of God given to man is a 'pre-constructed' text.

---

[7] Paul Ferguson, "The Battle Over Presuppositions On The Textual Issue" (*The Burning Bush*, Vol. 16, Nu. 1, Jan. 2010) p. 22-45.

Anyone who has bought an apartment or condo understands this concept. Very often the condo or apartment has a 'pre-constructed' covenant that one must agree to sign and to have notarized. With God's Covenant, man simply signs the agreement spiritually; that is, with his heart, mind, and soul (Mat. 22:37, Mark 12:30). When you come to God by faith, you are signing God's document because:

> "...faith *cometh* by hearing, and hearing by the word of God." Romans 10:17

A person cannot come to God except by faith which comes by hearing and accepting God's Covenant by faith (Heb. 11:6) through the Lord Jesus Christ.

> *But without faith it is impossible to please him: for he that cometh to God must believe that he is, and that he is a rewarder of them that diligently seek him. Hebrews 11:6*

The entire Biblical Covenant pertains to the Lord Jesus Christ. As we shall see, the Covenant is given by the Father who is in charge of operations, and the Son, who is the Administrator (1 Cor. 12:4-6). From one end to the other, the Covenant is about the Lord Jesus Christ. It is all to His glory (Jude, 1:25, Rev. 4:11). When you believe by faith in the Lord Jesus Christ, the Holy Spirit indwells, baptizes, and seals you until the day of redemption (Jn. 14:17, Acts 11:16, Eph. 4:12). He empowers you by grace with gifts to serve God both in this world and the world to come (Eph. 4:11, 1 Cor. 12:4).

God's Contract Filled With Precious Promises

Although this author thought he was the first to define the Bible as a "contract" with man, it turns out that many others have done so as well. Even as early as the second century after Christ, God's Words were being called a Contract. Tertullian (150-215 A.D.) said.

> "And what is "the voice of God" but the Word? And what is the Word but the Spirit"?[8] So much has been settled by the voice of God; such is **the contract** with everything which is born."[9] [my emphasis, HDW]

Without a doubt, the Bible is a Contract with man. It is absolutely complete. It is filled with promises, laws, statutes, and similar. God is one party and man is the other. God's *signature* on the Contract is with no less than the precious blood of His Son. God declares the Contract will not be altered or changed (Psa. 12:6-7, Psa. 119:89, Mat. 24:35, and many other places). Its preservation is attested to by over 5,500 manuscripts, many lectionaries, and many early versions of the Bible in other languages. Man and Satan have attempted to alter the *"precious promises,"* but they have been unsuccessful (Gen. 3:1-5, 2 Thess. 2:2).

> *2 Peter 1:4 Whereby are given unto us exceeding great and **precious promises**: that by these ye might be partakers of the divine nature, having escaped the corruption that is in the world through lust.*

The Covenant of God, i.e., the Bible, is absolutely necessary. Why? The Lord Jesus Christ says:

> *Matthew 4:4 But he answered and said, It is written, Man shall not live by bread alone, but by **every word** that proceedeth out of the mouth of God.*

If we do not have *"every word,"* God would be placing a requirement upon us that could not be fulfilled. He has promised us in many ways throughout His Covenant that His Words would be preserved. One of those ways is by the simple act of adding "salt," a

---

[8] Alexander Roberts; James Donaldson; A. Cleveland Cox, *The Ante-Nicene Fathers, Vol. I, II, III: Translations of the Writings of the Fathers Down to A.D. 325* (Logos Research Systems, Oak, Harbor, CA, 1997) p. 572.
[9] Ibid. Vol. III, p. 227.

preservative, to the sacrifices in the Old Testament. The typological meanings associated with the commandment are significant. First however, we need to examine various covenants more closely to gain an appreciation for how God uses covenants. The specific covenants within *The Covenant*, which are mentioned above (e.g. Abrahamic, Davidic, etc.), have great significance for understanding the promises of God, prophecy, and the specific covenant that this work is about.

Palestinian Covenant

The Palestinian Covenant is particularly important for grasping the understanding that **the land** God gave to His covenant people, the nation Israel, will one day belong to them. It is not dependent upon their behavior. It is unconditional. He will do it. The Palestinian Covenant reaffirms three very important statues:

1. Israel possesses the title deed to the land.
2. The promise cannot be abrogated for any reason.
3. The covenant amplifies the Abrahamic covenant and its stipulations will apply in spite of the bad behavior of the nation in the past or future.[10]

The Palestinian Covenant is an expansion of the Abrahamic Covenant (Gen. 12:1-3, and it is re-iterated or reinforced in many other passages in Scripture, just as the other covenants are.

Abrahamic Covenant

The Abrahamic Covenant is noted for its component parts. Essentially every author discussing this covenant lists three parts. But before they are enumerated, a little history is necessary. God changed

---

[10] J. Dwight Pentecost, *Things To Come, A Study in Biblical Eschatology* (Academie Books, Grand Rapid MI, Zondervan Publishing House, 1958, © 1964) p. 96.

Abram's[11] name to Abraham, meaning "the father of many nations" (Gen. 17:5). Abraham was the first patriarch and he is the ancestor of the nation Israel. He was the grandfather of Jacob, whose name was changed to Israel, meaning "prince of God" (Gen. 32:28). Jacob's twelve sons or their offspring would become the twelve princes of the twelve tribes of the nation Israel. Thus, the offspring of Abraham were destined to receive the promises made to Abraham through Isaac, Jacob, and finally Jacob's sons and grandsons. Keep in mind as you read the Scripture that use of terms such as 'father' does not necessarily mean a father-son relationship, but may mean simply the progenitor of physical descendants. In the Bible, Abraham was the "father" (ancestor) of the twelve princes of the tribes of Israel. The promises to Abraham pertain to the covenant people, Israel, as God promised in Genesis 12:1-3 and repeated to Abraham's physical descendants through Isaac and Jacob (Gen. 13:14-15, 17, 22:18). Esau was a physical descendant of Abraham, but he forfeited his birthright. Dr. Pentecost says:

> "...Esau was excluded because he was not eligible to receive the blessings since he was in unbelief. It will be observed that the birthright (Gen. 25:27-34) which Esau despised was the promise to which he was heir under the Abrahamic covenant. Since it rested on the integrity of God, Esau must be seen to be a man who did not believe God could or would fulfill His word."

Gentiles are grafted into the covenant promises by faith (belief). This is a blessing for Gentiles. The grafting is presented several ways in the Bible. The understanding is linked to the Lord Jesus Christ's description of Himself as the vine and His disciples as the branches. Paul describes the Gentiles as being grafted into the olive tree as a wild branch (John 15:1-5, Rom. 11:17-25). The olive tree represents typically the nation Israel in the Scriptures. As a result, Gentiles (and Jews), who believe in the Lord Jesus Christ and who are therefore members of

---

[11] Abram means 'high father.'

the body of Christ (the church) in this age, are grafted into the blessing of Israel through the church. Specifically, by faith, they receive the blessings of the Abrahamic Covenant through Christ reiterated throughout the Bible. Therefore, it behooves saints to understand the parts of the covenants into which we have been grafted and to comprehend their typological significance.

The Parts of the Abrahamic Covenant

The following are parts of the Abrahamic covenant: **1. Land, 2. Nation, and 3. Blessings.** These parts are found in several places in Scripture. The primary reference is Genesis 12:1-3:

> *[1]Now the Lord had said unto Abram, Get thee out of thy country, and from thy kindred, and from thy father's house,[1] unto a **land** that I will shew thee: [2] And I will make of thee a **great nation**, and I will bless thee, and make thy name great; and thou shalt be a **blessing**: [3] And I will bless them that bless thee, and curse him that curseth thee: and in thee shall all families of the earth be blessed.*

The phrase, "families of the earth," looks forward to the Lord Jesus Christ's incarnation and subsequent work of salvation through which the world would be blessed (Rom. 3:22-25, Jn. 3:16, 1 Jn. 2:2). The other parts of the Abrahamic covenant and its reiteration and expansions may be found throughout Scripture; for example, in Gen. 13:14-15, 17, 17:2-6, Deut. 30:3-5, Eze. 20:33-37, 42-44, Gen. 22:18, Jer. 31:31-40, Gal. 3:16, Heb. 8:6-13, 2 Sam 7:11, 13, 16 Jer. 31:35-37, 33:20-21. Anyone receiving the Lord Jesus Christ as their Saviour is grafted into the "blessing."

Typology

Many events, persons, and things in the Old Testament are a

"shadow" of things to come. The Scripture gives us permission to use this terminology.

> Colossians 2:17 "Which are a **shadow** of things to come; but the body is of Christ."
> Hebrews 10:1 "For the law having a **shadow** of good things to come, and not the very image of the things, can never with those sacrifices which they offered year by year continually make the comers thereunto perfect."

They are also called a *figure* or type of things to come. For example the lamb without spot or blemish sacrificed on the altar of burnt sacrifice in the Tabernacle of Moses or the Temple in Jerusalem is a *figure* of Christ. Therefore, John the Baptist called Jesus "the Lamb of God" (John 1:29). Similarly, the Tabernacle of Moses and the Ark of Noah were types of things to come, specifically the Lord Jesus Christ. As this work is not about the Tabernacle or Ark of Noah, the explanation or exegesis will not be presented here. However, the Bible makes it abundantly clear that typology is a teaching tool, particularly in the book of Hebrews. For example:

> Hebrews 9:8-9: [8] "The Holy Ghost this signifying, that the way into the holiest of all was not yet made manifest, while as the first tabernacle was yet standing: [9] Which was **a figure** for the time then present, in which were offered both gifts and sacrifices, that could not make him that did the service perfect, as pertaining to the conscience;"

The word *figure* in verse nine above is from the Greek word, παραβολη (parabole), which means a parable, proverb, similitude or figure (cf. Hosea 12:10). Jesus used parables in the New Testament (Mt. 13:34-35, Mk. 4:11). They can paint a "word-picture" to succinctly present a concept that would take many more words to explain. This is confirmed by the old adage, "a picture is worth a thousand words."

Also, Hosea tells us that God speaks to us by *similitudes*, which for the purpose of this work will be considered the same as a *figure*.

> Hosea 12:10 *"I have also spoken by the prophets, and
> I have multiplied visions, and used **similitudes**, by the
> ministry of the prophets."*

The word, "figures," found in Hebrews 9:24 below is from a different Greek word, αντιτυπος (antitupos), than the underlying Greek word in Hebrews 9:9.

> Hebrews 9:24 *"For Christ is not entered into the holy
> places made with hands, which are the **figures**
> [antitupos] of the true; but into heaven itself, now to
> appear in the presence of God for us:"* [my addition,
> HDW]

In the original language, the root words, "anti" and "tupos," clearly mean "corresponding to the type."

Many theologians use the terminology to follow. They call the "shadow" of the real person or thing to come, "the type." The **real** person or thing is called the antetype. It is a compound word; "ante" means "for" or "correspondence" or "in the place of" and "type" means "a "model" or "example" or "figure." Putting them together, the antetype would be the thing or person in place of the **example**; thus, the **real**. Therefore, the "lamb," sacrificed in the offerings of the Old Testament is the "type" and is the "shadow" of the Lord Jesus Christ, who is the **real** in the New Testament. The true Lamb is the antetype of the Old Testament, type, the lamb.

Furthermore, if the sacrifices in the Old Testament commanded by God are observed closely, one soon realizes that the various stipulated requirements accompanying the sacrifices either look forward to realization in the New Testament or they are representative of something.

For example, hardly any student of the Scripture does not understand that leaven represents sin throughout the Bible. Therefore the Feast of Unleavened Bread takes on added meaning. Similarly, the addition of the drink offering to sacrifices was commanded by God (Lev. 2; 6:14-23). It was offered with every blood and meat offering. Surely, God therefore intended a link between the "pouring out" (or sprinkling) of the blood and the meat (food) offering. One can only surmise, but the drink offering seems to represent (1) the Lord Jesus Christ "pouring out" Himself in total devotion or dedication to the Father's will (Jn. 5:30), and (2) the "pouring out" of His blood as the Lamb of God at Calvary (Mat. 26:28, Lk. 22:20). Similarly, the laying on of hands on the scapegoat, the honey, the wave offering, the heave offering, and the salt added to sacrifices represented something as a type. Many individuals, occurrences, and items in the Old Testament were types.

This author believes that the most important aspect of the typology of salt in the Bible and the requirement by God that it was to be added to the sacrifices has been overlooked. Most authors have identified possible typologies associated with "salt" (see chapter 14), but the most significant one has been missed in the opinion of this author. For example, consider Strong's definition:

217 halas: αλας *hal'-as* from 251; salt; **figuratively**, prudence:-- salt. (my emphasis, HDW)

Salt is not *figuratively,* prudence for certain. The purpose of this work is to try to understand why and how "salt" is used in Scripture. The writings of many throughout the centuries will be consulted.

The Covenant of Salt

God gave a commandment to the nation Israel concerning "salt," which was to be obeyed. It came in the form of a covenant. The stipulations of the covenant are interesting and significant.

In passages that present the covenant, the wording is difficult, fascinating and revealing. When understood by a consistent exegesis[12], the passages in Scripture that pertain to salt are much clearer. This is similar to understanding that leaven throughout Scripture is implicitly understood to represent sin.

Most teachers and authors garner the title of the covenant from Numbers 18:19. They call it *"a covenant of salt."* The covenant is identified in the following verse:

> *[Numbers 18:19] All the heave offerings of the holy things, which the children of Israel offer unto the Lord, have I given thee, and thy sons and thy daughters with thee, by a statute for ever: it is a **covenant of salt** for ever before the Lord unto thee and to thy seed with thee. [my emphasis]*

In another significant passage in Scripture where the word salt and covenant are linked, the covenant is identified by these words: *"the salt of the covenant"* (Lev. 2:13). This verse will take on far greater importance as we study other related passages.

> *[Leviticus 2:13] And every oblation of thy meat offering shalt thou season with salt; neither shalt thou suffer **the salt of the covenant** of thy God to be lacking from thy meat offering: with all thine offerings thou shalt offer salt.*

When the Covenant of Salt is understood, there are three component parts of this covenant, just as the Abrahamic Covenant has three parts. Like the Abrahamic Covenant, the parts of the Covenant of Salt are also expressed throughout Scripture. Some will immediately question whether the following verses are expressing the three parts of the covenant. Do not be too hasty in your conclusions! The reasons will become clear later as the exegesis is presented and explained over the

---

[12] Exegesis is the exposition of a text by inductive hermeneutics. Simply put, it is "an explanation or interpretation of a specific text, especially a religious one." (Encarta Dictionary).

remainder of this work. Briefly, salt represents the Words of God just as leaven represents sin. *"It is a covenant of salt,"* and the three parts are presented in various ways throughout the Bible. The three parts of the Covenant of Salt are found in Psa. 12:6-7.

> *[Psalm 12:6-7] The words of the Lord are **pure** words: as silver tried in a furnace of earth, purified seven times. [7] Thou shalt keep them, O Lord, thou shalt **preserve** them from this generation: **for ever.***

The parts are: **1. Pure, 2. Preserved, and 3. Eternal.** Other verses related to the covenant of salt are: Mat 5:18, 24:35, Isa. 30:8, Psa. 33:11, 119:89, 19:8, Col. 4:6, Mk 9:49-50, etc. This work is a literal, syntactic, lexical investigation of Covenant of Salt and *"the salt of the covenant;"* including the views of previous authors later on in this work concerning the concept of "salt" in Scripture and in the Church Age.

The Salt of the Covenant

Please note the word order in the phrase, *"the salt of the covenant of thy God."* As we shall see, typologically "salt" represents the very Words of Scripture. The understanding of the typology clarifies many passages.

Many authors have noted the difficult exegesis of passages such as Mark 9:49-50 and 2 Kings 2:20-21.

> *Mark 9:49-50 For every one shall be salted with fire, and every sacrifice shall be salted with salt. Salt is good: but if the salt have lost his saltness, wherewith will ye season it? Have salt in yourselves, and have peace one with another.*

> *2 Kings 2:20-21 "And he said, Bring me a new cruse, and put salt therein. And they brought it to him. And he went forth unto the spring of the waters, and cast the*

salt in there, and said, Thus saith the LORD, I have healed these waters; there shall not be from thence any more death or barren land."

The authors noting the difficulty will be presented in the last chapter. You may turn there first if you would like.

As we shall see, many authors have identified (1) salt as representative of the Words of the Bible and (2) the covenant as typologically referring to the Lord Jesus Christ. This typology often comes from a particular passage where the meaning is obvious but it is rarely transferred to other less obvious passages. Rather than being consistent in applying the typology throughout Scriptures, as in the case of leaven being a type of sin, many authors use the difficult passages to force their own particular theological position.

The explanation and application of these concepts to the difficult passages in Scripture associated with the terms will help simplify them. God does not try to make His Words complicated or difficult to understand for the believer. However, many author's explanations of numerous passages associated with salt have made them almost impossible to comprehend.

The Covenant in "the Salt of the Covenant"

In the unusually worded phrase, *"the salt of the covenant,"* what is the meaning of *"the covenant"*? This author believes that the sense of the phrase has been overlooked by many. The verses supporting this interpretation are the following. Isa 42:1-6 says,

Behold my servant, whom I uphold; mine elect, in whom my soul delighteth; I have put my spirit upon him: he shall bring forth judgment to the Gentiles. [2] He shall not cry, nor lift up, nor cause his voice to be heard in the street. [3] A bruised reed shall he not break, and the smoking flax shall he not quench: he shall bring forth judgment unto truth. [4] He shall not fail nor be discouraged, till he have set judgment in the *earth: and the isles shall wait for his law.[5] Thus saith God the Lord, he that created the heavens, and stretched them out; he that spread forth the earth, and that which cometh out of it; he that giveth breath unto the people upon it, and spirit to them that walk therein: [6] I the Lord have called thee in righteousness, and will hold thine hand, and will keep thee, **and give thee for a covenant** of the people, for a light of the Gentiles;[my emphasis]*

In light of the revelation from Scripture that the Lord Jesus Christ is *"a covenant,"* the unusually worded phrase, *"the salt (the Words of Scripture) of the covenant of thy God,"* takes on a much clearer and more significant meaning.

Summarized again, salt represents (1) the pure preserved, eternal Words of Scripture and, (2) in the phrase, the *"salt of the covenant of thy God,"* the covenant represents the Lord Jesus Christ. Putting the interpretation together in Leviticus 2:13, it indicates that those very Words come from *"the covenant of thy God,"* who is the *"word of God,"* the Lord Jesus Christ (John 1:1-2). The passage in Leviticus takes on a deeper meaning than previously considered by most (see chapter 14).

Also, this author believes that the exegesis extends to the very words of Scripture as preserved Words *forever* by the Covenant of the Lord thy God, the Lord Jesus Christ. That is His promise in many places in the Old Black Book. His *"words shall not pass away."* (see Psa. 12:6-7, Psa. 117, Mat. 24:35, Mark 13:31, Lk, 21:33, 1 Pe. 1:23-25). Salt is a preservative. An example is given in Judges 9:45 where it is used as a curing agent or a preserving agent to keep a city from being rebuilt.[13] It was used to keep the city in its destroyed state. Salt on meat keeps bacteria from growing. It acts as a preservative.

When the following phrase in Scripture reveals, *"by a statute forever: it is a covenant of salt forever,"* it should be understood that the promise is unconditional. It is a statute recorded in His Words. His

---

[13] Dr. John Gill (1690-1771), *Exposition of the Old and New Testaments,* Judges 9:45.

Words will remain **recorded** forever. It cannot relate to the sacrifice with salt itself, because we know that the sacrifices ceased from time to time in Israel's history. As a matter of fact, the sacrifices have ceased at the present time for almost two thousand years. But, we also know God promised to preserve His Words forever and the evidence is overpowering that He has and will!

Therefore, salt typologically represents (1) the Words of God (given by the "Covenant" who is the Lord Jesus Christ) and (2) the preserving of those Words, which establishes the eternal covenant and by extension to the entire Bible, which is an eternal covenant (q.v.).

Examples

Examples of these "statutes" maybe found in Numbers 18:19 and 2 Chron. 13:5.

> *[Numbers 18:19] All the heave offerings of the holy things, which the children of Israel offer unto the Lord, have I given thee, and thy sons and thy daughters with thee, by a statute for ever: it is a **covenant of salt** for ever before the Lord unto thee and to thy seed with thee. [2 Chron. 13:5] Ought ye not to know that the Lord God of Israel gave the kingdom over Israel to David for ever, even to him and to his sons by a **covenant of salt**?*

God's Words guarantee the promise.

This work hopes to clarify all of these things in the thirteen chapters to follow. This is just chapter 1. With the Lord's help, this author hopes to explain and inform the reader about the typology of salt, and to present the *"covenant of salt"* as an "unconditional" covenant of promise by God. By extension, the meaning also enhances His promises throughout the Bible to preserve His very Words, which testify of His promises. They will not fail. We are assured of this by the literal and partial fulfillment of many promises or prophecies in

Scripture.

The commandment to add salt to the sacrifices cannot simply be an inconsequential act without great meaning. God does not waste Words. He does not let any of *"his words fall to the ground"* (1 Sam. 3:19). Nor does He require His saints to waste time performing acts such as adding salt to the sacrifices without them having significant meaning. Consider the two ordinances of the church, baptism and the Lord's Supper. They have wonderful and important meanings.

Matthew 24:35 Heaven and earth shall pass away, but my words shall not pass away. (cf. Mark 13:31, Lk, 21:33)

CHAPTER 2

THE PRESERVATION OF GOD'S WORDS

In Chapter 1 of this work, the typology of salt in Scripture was briefly presented. There will be much more about his topic on the pages following. Since salt is a preservative, one feature of the typological addition of salt to the Old Testament sacrifices relates to preservation. The remarks to follow are related to the battle over the preservation of God's Words.

In these last days there is a concerted effort to usurp the belief in preservation of the Words of Scripture. It is based on the assumption, by rationalists, that in the manuscripts a significant number of God's words were corrupted, both intentionally and unintentionally! It is true that corruption has been a problem. The attempt to corrupt the Words of God began in the Garden of Eden and it has continued through the ages. A mountain of corruption was realized in the 1st and 2nd centuries, but a peak was achieved in the last three hundred to four hundred years, reaching a climax in the late eighteen hundreds. Two Anglican priests and professors in England, Westcott and Hort, were the main perpetrators of this false text in the mid to late eighteen hundreds in England. They constructed a false Greek Text based upon severely corrupted manuscripts that had been set aside for about fourteen hundred years.

However, God promised to preserve His Words (q.v.). Thus, a student of the history of the text can demonstrate a stream of manuscripts that goes back to the prophets and apostles. These are the Words of God that the Holy Spirit has watched over and preserved. These texts are the proper texts. It is a big stream, not just a trickle like the Alexandrian manuscripts supported by modernistic textual critics.

Therefore, there are two routes the Words of God have taken, one a wide stream and the other a trickle of water. The believer must have knowledge of this information and identify the two streams. The wide steam is *"living water."* It has continued unabated through the centuries.

The modern rationalists do not recognize or admit to the two separate routes the manuscripts (MSS) took. They believe man has been assigned the responsibility to *restore* the Scripture from *all* of the MSS or they elect to believe the false claim that the "oldest" manuscripts are the 'best." Those who believe that the literal words are lost insist on a re-evaluation of the doctrines of inerrancy, infallibility, and, finally, plenary inspiration.

Some, however, have not been swayed. The Masoretic scribes, who diligently copied God's words over the centuries, believed in the preservation of the Words of Scripture.[14] Certainly, many Church leaders throughout history have recognized and affirmed their preservation.[15] Additionally and most importantly, throughout the ages, Bible believers have accepted the concept of the preservation of God's Words because of clear, concise verses in the Scripture that affirm this truth (Psa 12: 6-7, Mat. 5:18, Psa 119:89, Psa 33:11, etc).

Many Corrupters of the Words of God

The Apostle Paul recognized that there were many corrupters (see 2 Cor. 2:17). Paul also cautioned the Thessalonians to be not troubled *"by word nor by letter as from us"* [2 Thes. 2:2]. Irenaeus, recognizing the number of corrupters, said, "Whosoever perverts the oracles of the Lord...he is the first-born of Satan"[16]; Marcion is noted for his

---

[14] D. A. Waite, Th.D., Ph.D., *Defending The King James Bible* (The Bible For Today, Collingswood, N.J.; 4th Printing, 1955) pp. 20-21.

[15] H. D. Williams, M.D., Ph.D., *The Lie That Changed The Modern World: A Refutation of the Modernist Cry: Poly-Scripturae* (Bible For Today, Collingswood, N.J.) pp.50-53.

[16] Alexander Roberts, D.D.; James Donaldson, LL.D; A. Cleveland Cox, *The Ante-Nicene Fathers, Vol. I, II, III: Translations of the Writings of the Fathers Down to A.D. 325* (Eerdmans Publishing Co., 1989, Logos Research Systems,

mutilation of Scripture, as was Tatian who wrote the *Diastessaron*.

A growing number of Church leaders have also recognized the *warfare* associated with this issue. The quite subtle war over the centuries has now become open combat. A few men have taken-up the mantle of defense to challenge the "authorities" or "scholars" who have either wittingly or unwittingly established an attack on the *doctrine* of preservation and the *mechanism* of preservation of Scripture. The "scholars" base their attack on the preserved words of God using one of the following opinions:

(1) God's Words have not been preserved, or

(2) Textual scholars must to do a lot of restoring, revising and editing of God's Words because they have not been perfectly preserved,[17] or

(3) Many of God's Words were lost for approximately 1400 years and rediscovered fortuitously by researchers. The manuscripts rediscovered are (called) the oldest and best,[18] or

(4) There is no "clear" statement by the Scriptures about **how** the Words were preserved.

Two Examples

Consider two examples of independent, fundamental Baptist professors who are denying or questioning Bible preservation. W. Edward Glenny, former professor at Central Baptist Seminary, Minneapolis, Minnesota, denied preservation in an article that

---

Oak, Harbor, CA, 1997) p. 34.

[17] This is false according to the Bible [Proverbs 22:20-21] "Have not I written to thee excellent things in counsels and knowledge, 21That I might make thee know the certainty of the words of truth; that thou mightest answer the words of truth to them that send unto thee? " and also according to scholars like D. A. Waite, Ph.D., ThD., who states, "There might be slight spelling variations or other small differences, but for all intents and purposes they did have the same manuscripts," for the traditional text (Textus Receptus). p. 36, *Foes of the King James Bible Refuted*, by Dr. Waite, available from BibleForToday.

[18] Dean John William Burgon addressed these issues in *Revision Revised.*

appeared in *The Bible Version Debate: The Perspective of Central Baptist Theological Seminary* (1997). The article is titled "The Preservation of Scripture." Consider the following plain statements,

> "The doctrine of the preservation of Scripture was first included in a church creed in 1647. As we have argued above IT IS NOT A DOCTRINE THAT IS EXPLICITLY TAUGHT IN SCRIPTURE, nor is it the belief that God has perfectly and miraculously preserved every word of the original autographs in one manuscript or text--type. It is a belief that God has providentially preserved His Word in and through all the extant manuscripts, versions and other copies of Scripture....not only does no verse in Scripture explain how God will preserve His Word, but THERE IS NO STATEMENT IN SCRIPTURE FROM WHICH ONE CAN ESTABLISH THE DOCTRINE OF THE PRESERVATION OF THE TEXT OF SCRIPTURE...it is also obvious from the evidence of history that GOD HAS NOT MIRACULOUSLY AND PERFECTLY PRESERVED HIS WORD IN ANY ONE MANUSCRIPT OR GROUP OF MANUSCRIPTS, OR IN ALL THE MANUSCRIPTS" (Glenny, *The Bible Version Debate*, pp. 93,95,99).

Glenny has stated his position plainly. He boldly denies that the Bible promises the preservation of Scripture. He explains away every passage that has traditionally been cited in support of preservation, including Ps. 12:7; 105:8; 119:89, 152, 160; Isa. 40:8; Matt. 5:18; and Matt. 24:35. At the same time he audaciously claims "a belief that God has providentially preserved His Word in and through **all** the extant manuscripts." That is an impossible position. There can be no "belief" without a Word from God. God has not declared that He would conceal His Words in all manuscripts or manuscripts still to be found; rather He has implied throughout the Bible that they would be available from generation to generation (e.g. Psa. 105:8).

"Faith cometh by hearing, and hearing by the word of God" (Rom 10: 17; see also Hebrews 11). If God had not explicitly promised

to keep His Word, we would not be able to have any faith whatsoever. If that were the case, then fathers of modern textual criticism would be correct in treating the Bible like any other book and applying their theories just as they do to the works of Homer or any other non-inspired writing.

Another example is James Price, a professor at Tennessee Temple University.

> "Dr. Price worked on the Old Testament portion of the New King James Bible, but he does not believe the Received Text is the preserved Words of God. The publishers of the New King James Bible implied in their advertisements that they revered the King James Bible and its Received Text and thus aimed to continue its legacy, but the men who did the translation actually believe the KJB is a weak, corrupt translation and they are committed to the critical Greek text (Alexandrian Text). In an e-mail to me dated April 30, 1996, Dr. Price said: "I am not a TR advocate. I am not at war with the conservative modern versions." In a more recent e-mail, Dr. Price stated that the Bible nowhere explicitly teaches that God will preserve the Scriptures. "One may infer the doctrine of preservation from statements in the Bible, but the explicit term 'preserve' (or its derivatives) is never used in the KJV of the written word of God" (price, e-mail, Dec. 20,2000). Whether or not the term "preserve" is in the Bible is neither here nor there. The question is, "Does the Bible teach that God will preserve the Scriptures?" When Price was understandably challenged for stating that God did not promise to preserve the Scriptures, he replied, "I know the passages that infer preservation, and I believe the doctrine. I just don't think that the Bible explicitly states how God preserved His word."[19] (my addition, HDW)

To those authorities that need 'science' to tell them "how"

---

[19] David Cloud, "Preservation Is Missing in Standard Works on Textual Criticism" (Fundamental Baptist Information Service, P.O. Box 610368, Port Huron, MI 48061, March 30, 1999).

everything is done by God, I ask the following questions: How did God "raise up" Lazarus? How did God part the Red Sea? How did Jesus heal the lepers, the blind, the lame, or those with palsy, bleeding, and dropsy? How is He going to accomplish the rapture? How did He raise up Jesus? Surely you believe He raised up Jesus? The implications of not believing He "raised up" Jesus are frightening, but He did not explain "how" He accomplished it. The need to explain everything God does portends a lack of faith. "How, how, how" is always the cry of "ye of little faith." Some things belong to the secrets of God (Deut 29:29).

This travesty of doubt or outright denial in preservation of the Words of God has been addressed on many scholarly levels by believers such as Dr. Edward F. Hills, Dr. D. A. Waite, Dr. Jack Moorman, Dr. David Brown, Dr. Kirk DiVietro, by many other authors of books and articles, and by a few organizations such as the Dean Burgon Society (DBS). However, their efforts have not been well received and most, I'm certain, feel like Elijah when he said, *"I, even I only, am left; and they seek my life, to take it away"* (1 Kings 19:14).

What some individuals have noted in the messages and comments at the Dean Burgon Society (DBS) Annual Meetings is the distinctively defensive position many speakers have taken. This is _not_ a criticism, but a point that needs to be made in light of this presentation. This presentation hopes to propose or add several offensive positions for those dealing with and defending the Received Texts (the Hebrew Masoretic text and the Greek Textus Receptus or Traditional Text) preserved through the priesthood of believers.

After a presentation at an annual Dean Burgon Society meeting concerning the affirmation or correctness of the translation of Psalm 12:6-7 by the KJB translators, after recalling the statements by Dr. Waite in his presentations and writings as regards preservation of the Words of God, and after recalling the many written messages over the years in the yearly compilation of the presentations in the DBS Message Books, this author has become convinced that God must have provided *an overarching covenant* that affirms or reinforces the idea of preservation. A covenant is a contract, and our God is a contract-making God. In the case of the Words of God, there must be an unconditional covenant, which 'covers,' establishes, or affirms not only all the covenants and their promises, but also, specifically, the concept of the preservation of the eternal Words of God. Is it not through His *preserved* Words, which are like a legal contract or covenant, and therefore, are Words which may not be changed, that He establishes the specific statements, conditions, or promises of a covenant?

A covenant[20] is a contract that is viewed in Scripture as either conditional or unconditional with its component parts, conditions, or promises. There are many promises throughout the Scriptures, stated in many different ways, concerning the promise of preservation of the Words of God. This author has documented over 100 verses relating to preservation.[21] Is it not reasonable to believe that the individual promises (or conditions, contingences, stipulations, agreement, conventions, declarations, intentions of the implied promise[22]) of preservation must be housed in an overarching covenant?

---

[20] Strong's (Heb. beriyth, from Hebrew 1262 (barah) (in the sense of *cutting* [like Hebrew 1254 (bara')]); a *compact* (because made by passing between *pieces* of flesh): confederacy, [con-] feder[-ate], covenant, league. and Gr. diatheke, from Greek 1303 (diatithemai); properly a *disposition,* i.e. (special) a *contract* (especially a devisory *will)* :- covenant, testament.)

[21] Please recall that in Scripture: keep, preserve, promise, forever, eternal, covenant, settled, etc. are words related to preservation.

[22] *Black's Law Dictionary.* West Publishing Company, 1979; 5th Edition.

Psalms 12:6-7 "The words of the LORD are pure words: as silver tried in a furnace of earth, purified seven times. Thou shalt keep them, O LORD, thou shalt preserve them from this generation for ever."

CHAPTER 3

COVENANTS OF PRESERVATION

This author has investigated for some time the concept of a covenant supporting the preservation of Scripture. Could it be true? He realizes this is deductive thinking, which can be hazardous. However, our conduct in a situation is determined by deductive considerations. For example, consider a phone call from a family member that your parents are in need of financial assistance because a source of income has been depleted (e.g. income from a mortgage owned by the parents that provided $900.00/month). How do we approach the issue of lending financial assistance? Deductively, we know the answer is in Scripture and we search the passages either by memory or by study. We find the answer in such verses as Exodus 20:12, Eph. 6:1, and **1 Tim. 5:4, 8**. Every situation an individual encounters in life is not detailed in the Bible. Therefore, an individual must deductively arrive at the way he will conduct himself. His actions are based upon clear verses in Scripture, which establish doctrine, and therefore, determines his response. The Bible is complete and the answers are there. We simply need to be familiar enough with the Bible to remain in the will of God by our actions, none of which are detailed for every situation with which a man finds himself confronted.

Therefore, could there be a covenant expressing the concept of preservation that has been missed or poorly understood that could be arrived at by deductive considerations? Needless to say, the Scripture attaches great importance to covenants. The phrase *"my covenant"* occurs 52 times in 49 verses.

Since God attaches such great importance to His Words in His Covenant, the Bible, and to their preservation (Deut. 29:9, Prov. 4:4, 7:1, etc.[23]), this author considered that a covenant as important as one

---

[23] The Hebrew word used in these passages is shamar ; a related Hebrew word

that affirms the preservation of His Words may be present. God knew that believers would be and are embroiled in the last days' battle for His Words. He always gives help, encouragement, and the necessary weapons for His 'children' to do battle. He is the Lord of Hosts.

Three Covenants Related to Preservation

This author has concluded that there is not only such a covenant, but that there are actually three covenants related to God's promise to preserve His Words.

(1) The Word, who is the Lord Jesus Christ, is affirmed in the Abrahamic Covenant as Abraham's descendant, which says *"in thee shall all families of the earth be blessed"* and that He is The Covenant [Isa. 42:6, 49:8]. It is the Lord Jesus Christ, the Covenant, who gave to man the *eternal* Words, the Covenant, that were given to Him by the Father (John 8:28, 17:8).

(2) The New Covenant expresses the preservation of the eternal Words written "within" expressed as *"my law"* in Jeremiah 31:32-33 and *"my covenant"* in Isaiah 59:21. In Scripture, *"the law"*[24] is sometimes an aphorism for all of the Scripture (Mat. 5:18, Jn. 1:17).

(3) The third covenant that reinforces preservation will be examined fully. It is *"a covenant of salt"* or *"the salt of the covenant of thy God."* The covenants have been there all the time. We will examine the last covenant through related passages and present research concerning this issue in the chapters to follow.

---

is natsar. They mean to watch over, protect, guard His Words. They are used hundreds of times in the Old Testament.

[24] Albert Barnes, *Notes on the New Testament, Explanatory and Practical*, *Notes on the Old Testament, Explanatory and Practical* (SwordSearcher, Broken Arrow, OK, Version 5.5, originally published 1832-1872). Barnes commenting on John 10:34 says *"In your law. The word law here, is used to include the Old Testament."*

Changing Meanings in a Postmodern Society

Before presenting the covenant in the chapters to follow, there are some points that need to be made concerning the selection of words used in these last days by spin, which is distortion of the truth to achieve an end. Many have shown that the deterioration in society has left marks that are unprofitable and deleterious on our way of life. Some have noted that the postmodern society has arrived with its Platonic reasoning,[25] its penchant for witchcraft,[26] its adoption of Eastern mystical thinking, its substitution of emotions and feelings for external truth (the Scriptures),[27] its denial of logic and reason, and its proclamation of "whatever." The postmodern society, also known as the "whatever" society, has one major feature. It is rejection of authority,[28] and in close pursuit are the symptoms outlined by Paul so beautifully in 2 Tim. 3:1-8:

> *"This know also, that in the last days perilous times shall come. 2For men shall be lovers of their own selves, covetous, boasters, proud, blasphemers, disobedient to parents, unthankful, unholy, 3Without*

[25] James H. Sightler, M.D., *A Testimony Founded Forever, The King James Bible Defended in Faith and History*: 2nd Edition; (Sightler Publications; Greenville, SC) Chapter 4, 6.

[26] David Cloud, 0 *Timothy* Magazine; Vol 12, Issue 9, 1995; "You can find anything on the Internet that you can find in the world outside of the Internet: New Age, Humanism, Pornography, Feminism, Ecumenism, Homosexuality, Communism, Witchcraft, White Supremacy, you name it. It is very much like visiting a book store or a library. Though there are many books which are edifying and helpful, there are many which are unhealthy to one's spiritual and moral life. To use a bookstore or a library--or the Internet-- properly requires discernment and maturity."

[27] Dr. Peter Masters, *East Wind Blows Wes;(0 Timothy* Magazine, Vol 5, Issue 7, 1988).

[28] H. D. Williams, M. D., *The Dean Burgon Society Messages From The 24th Annual Meeting (#12 in a Series,* (Bible For Today; Collingswood, NJ) p. 9-35. Also, *Hearing The Voice of God,* by Dr. Williams, chapter 6, "Postmodernism," published by The Old Paths Publications in 2008.

natural affection, trucebreakers, false accusers, incontinent, fierce, despisers of those that are good, 4Traitors, heady, highminded, lovers of pleasures more than lovers of God; 5Having a form of godliness, but denying the power thereof: from such turn away. 6For of this sort are they which creep into houses, and lead captive silly women laden with sins, led away with divers lusts, 7Ever learning, and never able to come to the knowledge of the truth. 8Now as Jannes and Jambres withstood Moses, so do these also resist the truth: men of corrupt minds, reprobate concerning the faith."

Now let us examine the major points related to the postmodernist. There is a specific "word" for which the postmodern society seems to have absolutely no respect. Before I give you the word, let me give you some facts.

Some Facts

1. Our society has lost its integrity. Just 50 years ago, the attribute of honesty was still respected by most individuals, but not any more. The word integrity is derived from the Latin root *integer*. Most of you will recognize this as a mathematical term applied to a whole number. Therefore we can talk about a person who has integrity as being whole. A person with integrity is not divided, acting differently in different circumstances, and is living righteously.

> "A person of integrity is the same person in private that he or she is in public."[29]

A person "pure in heart" has integrity and is undivided and not double minded. James said, "A double minded man *is* unstable in all his ways" (Jam. 1:8).

---

[29] Kerby Anderson, B.S., M.F.S. (Yale), M.A., (Georgetown), *Integrity*, www.probe.org/docs/integrity.html (last accessed 2003).

2. The opposite of integrity is corruption. Corruption is like rust. It spreads and destroys unless measures are instituted to control it. There are innumerable studies that have been done to demonstrate the corruption and loss of integrity in our society. I am hearing reports that this phenomenon is worse in other nations around the world. The facts I have, that are related to integrity in this country, are outlined in the following comments.

A book, *The Day America Told The Truth,* by Patterson and Kim and published in 1991, related some astonishing facts. The authors conducted a survey using a technique which guaranteed anonymity of the respondents. These astounding results were amazing! The outcome is summarized here:

3. There was no moral *foundation* or code that America uses any longer. The Ten Commandments were believed by only thirteen [13 %] of Americans in 1990. Only forty-five percent [45%] of the respondents believed in five (5) of the Ten Commandments in the same year. This is completely contrary to the moral code of America as recent as the 1950's.[30] This date correlates with the release of the RSV in 1952, the NASV in 1960, the NEB in 1961 and the NIV in 1973. These dates also show a relationship to the sudden acceleration in facts and figures related to crime in this nation that was presented to the DBS last year.[31]

4. "Lying has become an integral part of American culture, a trait of the American character. We lie and don't even think about it. We lie for no reason.[32] Patterson and Kim's exhaustive research reveals that ninety-one percent [91 %] of us lie regularly--conscious, premeditated lies. They conclude, "Lying has become a cultural trait in America.

---

[30] Ibid, p. 2.
[31] "The Lie That Changed The Modern World, A Demonstration of the Abandonment of 'Final Authority': Its Consequences Spiritually and Physically," *The Dean Burgon Society Messages From the 24th Annual Meeting.* p. 9-35.
[32] Kerby Anderson, B.S., M.F.S. (Yale), M.A., (Georgetown), *Integrity,* www.probe.org/docs/integrity. html, p. 2 (last accesses 2003).

Lying is embedded in our national character. We are in national disgrace."[33]

4. They found the respect for the institution of marriage is gone, the protestant work ethic has been scrapped, and Americans use a perverted set of new commandments.

5. George Barna concurs with the conclusions of Patterson and Kim. He said in his book, *Boiling Point*, that moral anarchy has arrived in the United States. He reports in his surveys that there is no respect for absolutes, the clergy, Christianity, personal holiness, church loyalty, or God.

6. The Josephson Institute of Ethics reported their findings in *Survey Documents Decade of Moral Deterioration: Kids Today Are More Likely To Cheat, Steal and Lie Than Kids 10 Years Ago.* "A survey of 12,000 high school students showed that students admitting they cheated on an exam at least once in the past year jumped from 61% in 1992 to 74% in 2002; the number who stole something from a store within the past 12 months rose from 31% to 38%, while the percentage who say they lied to their teachers and parents also increased substantially."[34] We can't lay all the blame on the children when 91 % of all Americans lie, cheat, and/or steal.

The Word Promise No Longer Has Integrity

7. The word that has lost its 'integrity' when used is **promise**. This teacher once held a class on finances at a Baptist church. In order to plan, he sent a sign-up list around to the various adult classes. Almost 70 people signed up. A note on the sign-up sheet stated that it was for planning purposes for refreshments. One person showed up for the class.

---

[33] Charles Crismier, J. D., President, SAVE AMERICA; *Preserve Us A Nation*: (Vision House Publishing, Inc., Gresham, Oregon, 1994) p. 85.
[34] Michael Josephson, Josephson Institute of Ethics, p. 1.
www.josephsoninstitute.org /survey2002 / survey2002-pressrelease.htm (last accessed in 2003).

Can anyone say the promise of wedding vows, such as the following, is being kept?

> I, _____, take thee _____, to be my lawfully wedded wife/husband, and before God and these witnesses I **promise** to be a faithful and true wife/husband."

A promise in this postmodern age means nothing. I frequently hear others comment on the following 'promise,' "I promise you I'll be there." What a laugh that statement has become. Therefore, when "the *promise* of the preservation of God's Words" found in numerous places in Scripture is encountered, most do not accept it, as if God were a man (Num. 23:19).

Although the comments to follow by this author will have relatively little if any impact, the necessity and desire to make them remain. For anyone holding a postmodernist philosophy, a *promise* is usually null and void the moment the vow or promise is made. The postmodernist has no desire for truth outside of himself. Everything is 'relative.' Nothing is absolute, including the Words of God. He has been completely indoctrinated by the postmodern world system, by society, by educational systems, by "science falsely so called" (1 Tim 6:20) and sadly, by many post-denominational[35] churches. In light of the preceding, Luke's record of Jesus' Words becomes strikingly real. *"And he said unto him, If they hear not Moses and the prophets, neither will they be persuaded, though one rose from the dead."* [Luke 16:31]

This author contends that a different tactic must be used to deal with the postmodern and post-denominational society. The proposal is

---

[35] *Beware of Ecumenism Flying Under the Flag of "Revival",* O'Timothy Magazine, Vol. 9, Issue 6, 1992; Way of Life Literature, Port Huron, MI. "Glenn Sheppard, senior associate for prayer for the Lausanne Committee for World Evangelization, agrees with Dawson. ..."I believe we are entering a post-denominational era," he theorizes, expressing a conviction that various churches and ministries will engage in a deeper level of cooperation as renewal efforts increase."

based on Scriptural concepts. If we carry the banner of Truth, the preserved Words of God in sixty-six canonical books, then let us set out a pro-active plan.

CHAPTER 4

THE POSTMODERN SOCIETY AND PRESERVATION

A Strategy is Needed

A strategy to deal with the postmodern society is needed. The postmodernists disregard the Truth, which is the preserved, inerrant, infallible Words of God in Hebrew, Aramaic, and Greek given by inspiration from a Person, the Lord Jesus Christ (Jn. 8:32, 14:6, 17:17) by the Holy Spirit. The major theme encompassing postmodern philosophy is **"the rejection of certainty."**[36]

Therefore, any call to listen to the Covenant of God, the Bible, which is a Promise (see the definitions in the Preface), is rejected in favor of feelings, mysticism, and humanistic philosophy. The attitude of the postmodern world completely ignores Colossians 2:8:

> *"Beware lest any man spoil you through philosophy and vain deceit, after the tradition of men, after the rudiments of the world, and not after Christ."*
> *Colossians 2:8*

Because the postmodernist does not abide in the truth (Jn. 8:44), he immediately rejects the theme of the promises running repeatedly throughout. That theme is the high honour that God has for His Son and for His saving Words (Mat. 3:17, 17:5, Jn. 1:1-2, Mat. 4:4, Rom. 10:17, 2 Pe. 1:17, etc.). The Lord expresses it in every way possible, including various covenants, that point to the ability of the Words to

---

[36] John MacArthur, *The Truth War, Fighting for Certainty in an Age of Deception* (Thomas Nelson, Nashville, TN, 2007) p. 12.

save a person from everlasting hell (Gen. 12:1-3, Mat. 10:28, Psa. 12;6-7, Psa. 117, Mat. 4:4, 24:35, Acts 2:31, 1 Pet. 1:23-25, Rev. 20:13). Hopefully, this work will help one or two to see God's promises proclaimed in a way not generally noticed; *"the salt of the covenant of thy God."* Perhaps, understanding and seeing God proclaim His Truths in ways not generally taught, the postmodernist or the backslidden believer will turn to the only Truth. In the meantime, even though this problem is frustrating to solid believers in the Words of God, we must deal with it with great longsuffering. This 'way' is amply demonstrated by the way the Lord Jesus Christ dealt with the Samaritan woman at the well. There, standing before that lost fornicating woman, was the God of creation. Yet, that God of all creation pointed the woman to her sin and to truth in a gentle loving way. May we all do the same (John 4:4-41).

A Good Warfare

The strategy to deal with this perplexing endtime problem of *uncertainty* must be characterized by an active patience and *"a good warfare"* (1 Tim. 1:18). The Scripture sometimes pictures a *passive* waiting or *"longsuffering"* for the resolution of life's trials. For example, in Galatians 5:22, one component of the fruit of the Spirit is longsuffering. The Greek word used is macrothumia. This is characterized in Strong's Concordance as *longanimity,*[37] that is, (objectively) *forbearance* or (subjectively) *fortitude, meaning* longsuffering or patience. It is characterized *in Practical Word Studies in the New Testament* as

> "1. Patience never strikes back. Common sense tells us that a person who is attacked by others could strike back and retaliate. *But* the Christian believer is given…the power to be patient with the…person for a

---

[37] Strong's number 3115: from the same as 3116; longanimity, i.e. (objectively) forbearance or (subjectively) fortitude:--longsuffering, patience.

long, long time."[38]

The ability to store up wrath. **This is longsuffering that is passive**.

In other places, the Scripture emphasizes patience that is *active*. Colossians 1: 11 says:

> *"Strengthened with all might, according to his glorious power, unto all patience and longsuffering with joyfulness;"*

Practical Word Studies characterizes patience, Greek hupomonen, in this verse as "not passive; it is *active.*" It is not the spirit of man that sits back and puts up with the trials of life, taking whatever may come. Rather, it is the spirit that stands up, faces the trials of life, and actively goes about conquering and overcoming them. When trials confront a person who is truly justified, he is stirred to arise and face trials head on. He immediately sets out to conquer and overcome them. Often, he knows God is allowing the trials in order to teach him more and more patience (endurance)."[39] Paul tells us in Romans 12:18 "If it be possible, as much as lieth in you, live peaceably with all men." Perhaps the time has come for many of us to peacefully "strateuomai," strategize or war, as Paul told Timothy:

> *"This charge I commit unto thee, son Timothy, according to the prophecies which went before on thee, that thou by them mightest war [strateuomai] a good warfare;" 1 Tim 1:18 (my addition, HDW).*

> *"Thou therefore endure hardness, as a good soldier of Jesus Christ. [4] No man that warreth entangleth himself with the affairs of this life; that he may please*

---

[38] *Practical Word Studies In The New Testament. Vol. 2. L-Z. The Outline Bible* (Leadership Ministries World, Chattanooga, TN) ISBN 1-57407-108-4; 1998, p. 1510.
[39] Ibid. p.1510.

him who hath chosen him to be a soldier." 2 Tim. 2:3-4

Every man, church, pastor, missionary, teacher, or lay believer needs a strategy or a war plan, based on the realization we are "soldiers," and based on Paul's end time prophecies:

> *"This know also, that in the last days perilous times shall come. For men shall be...Ever learning, and never able to come to the knowledge of the truth." [2 Tim 3:1,7]*

If we believe war-times are here, then we need an *active,* patient, peaceful plan. I will hasten to add that the activity most needed is prayer, which anyone in the ministry for any length of time knows to be true.

Jesus' brother James reflects on passivity or activity by stating:

> *Yea, a man may say, Thou hast faith, and I have works: shew me thy faith without thy works, and I will shew thee my faith by my works. James 2:18*

We need to be persistently working on the *warfare* surrounding the preservation of God's Words with a strategy and with every weapon the Scripture allows.

CHAPTER 5

THE WORD PROMISE
HAS LOST ITS IMPORT

The Need to Appropriate
the Bible as a Legal Document

A proposal or strategy for the battle includes the choice of words used to support a position. This choice takes on great significance. In fact, it is critical in a postmodern world, which lies, cheats, and steals more than any other generation.

Perhaps, as part of the war plan or strategy, the word *"promise"* should be used less often or even dropped when referring to "the promise of preservation of His Words." Even though the word promise is frequently used in Scripture, its meaning to the post-modernists is nil.[40] A promise carries no weight in this postmodern world. In the postmodernist's opinion a promise has no 'legal' weight behind it. In other words, there is no punishment in the majority of cases for breaking a promise. In our world today, promises, whether made by politicians, individuals, organizations, governmental bodies, or even God in the Bible are perceived to be broken without consequences. Most have no moral qualms about breaking a promise and most are totally ignorant of the Biblical injunctions against doing so. A promise breaker is a liar. The Bible has harsh words for individuals who are liars.

The only deterrents to total anarchy in this country and in the world today are the *legal* authorities and the threat of imprisonment by

---

[40] Promise or a cognate of the word is used 117 times in 111 verses in Scripture.

the courts for breaking the laws of a nation. Although we should not determine our position based on man's attitudes, we can alter the use of words, not definitions, to draw attention to the _legal_ position of the Bible in regards to the preservation of His very Words. This may seem to be trite to some reading this work, but please read a little more.

One of the premises of this book is that the position of Scripture in regards to preservation is one of a contract or covenant; it should not be viewed as simply a promise as defined by the modern world; that is, something that has no consequences if it is broken.

The "Ark of the Covenant" is not called the "Ark of the Commandments" in the Bible for similar reasons. Even though the Ark contained the Ten Commandments, or Statutes, or Laws that constituted a covenant, it was not called the Ark of the Commandments. In addition, the Ark was the mercy seat of "The Covenant" who is the Lord Jesus Christ (briefly explained previously and will be expanded below). He is a Covenant for 'all the people of the world.' We dare not call Him the promise for 'all the people of the world' for fear that they will ignore the true promise (covenant) of a Holy God.

This author believes that there is a legal covenant of the preservation of His words conjoined with the Covenant, the Lord Jesus Christ. It is a legal, contractual position of Scripture. In addition, many have broken that contract. Therefore, they are in jeopardy of legal action against them by the Lord of Hosts. He said very clearly in Matthew 5: 19:

> _"Whosoever therefore shall break [luo] one of these least commandments, and shall teach men so, he shall be called the least in the kingdom of heaven: but whosoever shall do and teach them, the same shall be called great in the kingdom of heaven."_

Just before Jesus made this momentous statement, He presented an expanded requirement for believers in the Beatitudes (Mat 5:3-11). Although the beatitudes have the most significance for the dispensation of the millennium, the spirit of the passage should be practiced by believers in this dispensation.

Jesus also commented on the preservation of the smallest parts of a word of Scripture in verse 18 of Mat. 5. The import is that anyone who *"breaks [luo] one of these"* by alterations of the Words (1) by addition, subtraction, or changing (see John 10:34-35 below), **or** (2) by deeds or actions, *"shall be called least."* I fear there are many brothers and sisters in the household of believers who have not appropriated the meaning of Mat. 5:19, or the meaning of dozens of other verses, and they are in danger of being called *"the least."*

John also quotes Jesus as having said the *"scripture cannot be broken."* On the occurrence of this statement He was referring to the Hebrew judges who interpret God's law and justice.[41] He called them "gods" in Psa. 82:6.

> *Jesus answered them, Is it not written in your law, I said, ye are gods? 35If he called them gods, unto whom the word of God came, and **the scripture cannot be broken;** [John 10:34-35]*

Jesus was referring to **the** very **letters of Scripture**, making the point that if Scripture uses the word "gods" to refer to those magistrates in authority, He had even greater authority. Therefore the stones, which the Jews picked up to throw at Him for blasphemy, were dropped because Jesus had not said anything contrary to the Scriptures. He could not be accused of blasphemy because He, who had even greater authority, called himself *"the Son of God."*

Conclusion

The words of God are a **covenant** and cannot be "broken." Therefore, this author believes the following statement should be used

---

[41] *The King James Study Bible,* (Thomas Nelson Publisher, Nashville); Note on Jn 10:34; p.1630.

less, *"the promise of the preservation of His words."* Instead, the phrase, *"the covenant of the preservation of His words"* should be used. This is supported by the positions and information on covenants to be presented below and by the reasons given above. We should say God covenanted to preserve His Words. A covenant is viewed as a legal position by most individuals. Truly, God has established a legal position for His Words. They are absolute. They are weightier than any words ever recorded. They must not be viewed as a promise to be "broken."

CHAPTER 6

COVENANT TERMINOLOGY

The word "covenant" should not be objectionable to either covenant or dispensational theological positions. It is used by both positions. Both theological camps claim the importance of "covenants." Keith Mathison relates,

> "Dispensationalists and others also recognize covenants, the biblical covenants, but they cannot be recognized as covenant theologians."[42]

Although Charles Ryrie does not agree with the major covenants proposed by covenant theologians and neither does this author, Ryrie does agree that

> "other covenants are specifically revealed and in great detail ... "[43]

Ryrie means the covenants specifically dealt with in this work, such as the Abrahamic, Davidic, Palestinian, and New Covenants clearly revealed in the Bible and briefly discussed previously.

John Gerstner relates,

> "What the dispensationalist means by a dispensation is, in a formal sense, what covenant theologians mean by covenant."[44]

---

[42] Keith A. Mathison, *Dispensationalism Rightly Dividing the People of God*, (Presbyterian and Reformed Publishing Co.; Phillipsburg, New Jersey; 1995), p. 4.

[43] Charles C. Ryrie, *Dispensationalism Today;* (Moody Press, Chicago; 1965); p. 1990.

[44] John H. Gerstner, *Wrongly Dividing The Word Of Truth*, (Wolgemuth and

The word "covenant" is here to stay.

As previously mentioned, covenants in Scripture are recognized by theologians as conditional[45] or unconditional.[46] The covenants someone lists are dependent on his/her theological position. Covenant theologians generally list a "Covenant of Grace" and a "Covenant of Works." They maintain that the Church *replaced* Israel; they emphasize soteriology; and they tend toward allegorization of Scripture. They do not list a "Covenant of Preservation," but they do recognize other covenants such as the Noahic, Abrahamic, Palestinian, Davidic, and New Covenants. Covenant theologians do not seem to be as inclined to support the concept of the preservation of the words of God. The reason for this may be their overall tendency toward the deductive approach to Scripture and the allegorization of major parts of it.

Dispensationalists list the major covenants such as the Noahic, Abrahamic, Palestinian, Davidic, and New Covenants. In contrast to covenant theologians, they do not emphasize soteriology over the purpose of creation, which Scripture indicates is to the glory of God (Rev. 4: 11).[47] Dispensationalists do not believe the Church replaced Israel. Hermeneutically, they approach the Scripture literally and inductively, but they do allow for similes, metaphors, personification, hyperbole, parables, similitudes, etc. They do not tend to "spiritualize" the Scripture, but look to the plain literally sense of a passage. Dispensationalists seem to be more inclined to believe in the preservation of the very words and letters of Scripture.

However, this author has noted that some five point Calvinists and Reformed theologians are adamant that God has preserved His

---

Hyatt Publishers, Inc.; Brentwood, Tenn., 1991) p. 265.

[45] Adamic, Edenic, Noahic, and Mosaic Covenants are classical conditional covenants or "if...then" covenants.

[46] The Unconditional Covenants include the Abrahamic Covenant and its subdivisions; Palestinian, Davidic, and New Covenants.

[47] Rev. 4:11 "Thou art worthy, 0 Lord, to receive glory and honour and power: for thou hast created all things, and for thy pleasure they are and were created."

Words. A five point Calvinist stresses (1) the total depravity of man, to the point that he cannot choose God, but that God chooses him as one of the elect, (2) the unconditional election of a man for salvation, (3) the limited atonement by the work of the Lord Jesus Christ to the elect, (4) the irresistible grace of God, which means the elect cannot resist God, and (5) the perseverance of the saints. However, this author is quick to add that there is such a wide variation in the way Covenant theologians define or approach the five points that a blanket application of the usual descriptions to a Calvinist or Reformed theologian is not realistic.

*Ephesians 1:10 "That in the **dispensation** of the fulness of times he might gather together in one all things in Christ, both which are in heaven, and which are on earth; even in him:"*

*Ephesians 3:2 "If ye have heard of the **dispensation** of the grace of God which is given me to you-ward:*

*Colossians 1:25 "Whereof I am made a minister, according to the **dispensation** of God which is given to me for you, to fulfil the word of God";*

*1 Corinthians 9:17 "For if I do this thing willingly, I have a reward: but if against my will, a **dispensation** of the gospel is committed unto me."*

CHAPTER 7

ANOTHER LOOK
AT THE NEW COVENANT

There are two covenants, the New Covenant and the Covenant of Salt, which are not unusually mentioned by covenant theologians and dispensationalists, but only certain aspects of each one are discussed. It depends on whether you approach the Scripture as a covenant theologian or a dispensationalist as to the aspect emphasized.

Both positions usually discuss only one aspect of the New Covenant. Both camps mention the Covenant of Salt but not nearly as often as the New Covenant. Perhaps the Covenant of Salt is not discussed because many authors document difficulty understanding the use of the word salt in Scripture. This author believes some covenants support the preservation of God's Words and most dispensationalists do. A closer look at the Covenant of Salt will be presented after a review of the New Covenant.

Although this paper is a new look at an old covenant, the Covenant of Salt, a brief look at the New Covenant is appropriate. It is appropriate because it is also a covenant that supports the use of the word "covenant" above the use of the word "promise" when referring to the preservation of His Words as discussed in this work. The tenet usually mentioned by both camps in the New Covenant is the indwelling of the Holy Spirit. However, Isaiah and Jeremiah present a second aspect of the New Covenant that for some reason is placed "on the back burner." Isaiah 59:21 says:

> "As for me, this is my covenant with them, saith the Lord; My spirit that is upon thee, **_and my words_** which

*I have put in thy mouth, shall not depart out of thy mouth, nor out of the mouth of thy seed, nor out of the mouth of thy :seed's seed, saith the Lord, from henceforth and **for ever**."*

God said through Isaiah *"my covenant"* has certain aspects that are related to *"my spirit"* **and** *"my words."* Note that 'words' is plural. Note three aspects (again) related to His Words. He said (1) that He will *"put"* them, (2) that they will *"not depart,"* and (3) that they are *"for ever"*!

God speaking through Jeremiah gave the three parts it in a similar way.

*"Behold, the days come, saith the Lord, that I will make **a new covenant** with the house of Israel, and with the house of .Judah: (32) Not according to the covenant that I made with their fathers in the day that I took them by the hand to bring them out of the land of Egypt; which my covenant they brake, although I was an husband unto them, saith the Lord: (33) But this shall be the **covenant** that I will make with the house of Israel; After those days, saith the Lord, I will **put mv law in their inward parts, and write it in their hearts**; and will be their God, and they shall be my people." [Jer.31:31-33]*

Obviously Isaiah's quote of God saying "my words" in Isa 59:21 is the equivalent of Jeremiah's "my law" in verse 31:33. Please notice in the following passage that He also said in Jeremiah 32:39-40 that it would be "forever" and "an everlasting covenant." This author also believes that the passage in Jeremiah meant *God's Words* are the "one way" because they all about Jesus who is the only way to heaven (Jn. 14:6). And, *my fear* is not only a reverence for God, but it is also a reference to the fear of Isaac (Gen. 31:42, 53), who is the pre-incarnate Jesus Christ. He dwells within the believer in this dispensation and the one to come along with the Father and the Spirit (Jn. 14:17, 23).

*Jer. 32:39-40 And I 'will give them **one heart**, and **one***

> *way*, *that they may fear me **for ever**, for the good of them, and of their children after them: (40) And I will make an **everlasting covenant** with them, that I will not turn away from them, to do them good; but I will put **my fear** in their hearts, that they shall not depart from me."*

God said through His prophets, Isaiah and Jeremiah, that He would **preserve His words forever** in their hearts and that this aspect of His **Covenant** would be **everlasting**. God's Words are forever settled in heaven [Psa 119:89], and not one jot or tittle will ever disappear [Mat. 5:18], and man should live by every word that proceeds out of the mouth of God [Mat. 4:4]. This is **an** "everlasting covenant" of the preservation of God's Words, because it is preserved **in** His words. The "everlasting covenant" in Scripture is also Jesus Christ, (see below), His Gospel, and His words, which are all contained in the expression "a covenant of salt." Therefore, salt typifies or symbolically represents the preserved, pure Words of God.

> *Numbers 18:19: "All the heave offerings of the holy things, which the children of Israel offer unto the Lord, have I given thee, and thy sons and thy daughters with thee, by **a statute for ever**: it is a **covenant of salt for ever** before the Lord unto thee and to thy seed with thee."*

The "statute" is His Words. They preserve **forever in Scripture**, the Covenant of Salt, which is the Covenant that typologically represents the preserved, pure Words in Hebrew, Aramaic, and Greek. Even if the offerings cease, which they did in 70 A.D. when the Roman General Titus destroyed the Temple in Jerusalem, the statute is preserved **in** His words, "the salt" of the covenant, forever. God was assuring the Levites that the heave offering was a gift to them by His words, which are forever, and the gift was therefore a covenant of salt, preserved in His words. The remainder of this book explains this position. It is a fact that Ezekiel reports a rebuilt Temple in the millennium when the offerings or sacrifices will be reinstituted. Most theologians believe this will be a memorial type offering in remembrance for all that has gone before. It will not look forward to Calvary, rather it will look back.

CHAPTER 8

A SIGNIFICANT PASSAGE

Colossians 4:6 "Let your speech be alway with grace, seasoned with salt, that ye may know how ye ought to answer every man."

After reviewing many books and writings by other authors, this author believes the Covenant of Salt has been only partially understood. This author believes the primary exegesis of the Covenant of Salt is this: The salt is typologically the preserved, pure, inerrant, infallible, eternal Words of God that were recorded in heaven and given to the prophets and apostles to record as revelation as Hebrew, Aramaic, and Greek Words. Man would have absolutely no clue as to many truths if he did not have the revelation of God recorded in sixty-six books.

The only Biblical, eternal things are: Heaven, Hell, Jesus Christ, His Words (the Bible), the Father, the Holy Spirit, the saints, angels, and unbelievers in Hell. The eternal gospel will one day reach complete fulfillment and will no longer be efficacious although it will remain recorded in His Words, forever, as a Covenant of Salt. This Covenant metaphorically represents His Words, which are pure, purified, and perfect, received from the Word, who is the Lord Jesus Christ. This author believes the consistent full understanding of the covenant was *"for such a time as this"* (Esther 4:14) when men shall hold in low esteem the **preserved** words of life in the Hebrew, Aramaic, and Greek texts.

Men through the ages have characterized the Covenant of Salt in many different ways (see the research below). This author believes the most significant aspect has not been fully appreciated. If commentators recognized the meaning in one passage, they did not transfer the concept to other passages. Yes, the Covenant of Salt does speak of preservation, purity, and eternality, but it speaks of much more. If one traces the word, salt, through the Scripture, the exegetical meaning of its use becomes more apparent. This is a literal, lexical, syntactic analysis of the passages dealing with salt and the Salt Covenant. A significant passage that bears on this meaning is Colossians 4:6. Paul said:

> *"Let your speech be alway with grace, seasoned with salt, that ye may know how ye ought to answer every man."*

In this passage, the Holy Spirit used the phrase *"seasoned with salt."* Many authors have written that the phrase is defining or modifying grace. This author believes that Paul, who was the Hebrew of Hebrews, a Pharisee, the member of the Sanhedrin, who sat at the feet of Gamaliel (Acts 7:58-22:3, Phil. 3:5), and who was very familiar with the Old Testament, recorded the Words from the Holy Spirit to indicate something far different. The Spirit was indicating the following four (4) ideas to believers:

1. *"Let your speech [Gr. logos] be alway with grace"*: By the use of these Words, the Spirit was indicating that a believer should "alway" be with the divine influence of the saved heart; that is, full of graciousness or gratitude for the unmerited favor extended to sinners.[48] That is the meaning of grace [G. charis] in this passage.

2. The phrase *"seasoned with salt"* means (a) there is no way for anyone's speech to be seasoned with "salt" unless their words are sprinkled with the pure, preserved, engrafted Words of God used with liberty. They most flow from the heart of a saved person. The Words of the *"one shepherd"* are like "goads" to people, but we are to use them

---

[48] **GS485** charis From G5463; *graciousness* (as *gratifying*), of manner or act (abstract or concrete; literal, figurative or spiritual; especially the divine influence upon the heart, and its reflection in the life; including *gratitude*): -acceptable, benefit, favour, gift, grace (-ious), joy liberality, pleasure, thank (-s, - worthy).

with grace and kindness. Ecclesiastes 12:11 says:

> The **words** of the wise are as goads, and as nails fastened by the masters of assemblies, which are **given from one shepherd**.

The *Geneva Translation Notes,* John Gill's *Exposition of the Whole Bible*, and John Calvin's *Institutes of the Christian Religion* have identified salt as "the incorruptible word" and the "word of Christ" respectively, in other passages of Scripture.[49] However, they did not transfer the typology to passages such as Col. 4:6:

> Let your speech be alway with grace, seasoned with salt, that ye may know how ye ought to answer every man. Colossians 4:6

Those authors who have typologically identified "salt" as grace have probably missed the typology Paul was using in this passage. We are to hide His words in our hearts (Psa. 119:11). One purpose of this command is to be able to used them in our speech. We are to season our speech with "salt."

"Seasoned" is a Passive Participle

The word *"seasoned"* is a passive participle modifying "speech." It is not defining "grace." The Spirit was indicating by the use of the passive voice that the Words of God affect one's speech in a way that man has no control over or cannot affect. God's Words are so powerful that they can cause a man to be saved. In other words, when a man uses God's Words, it is "seasoned speech" by God's Words (salt), which have been purified seven times (Psa. 12:6-7). Now that is true seasoning.

---

[49] See Geneva Translation Notes, Mark 9:49; and John Gills Exposition of the Whole Bible, Mark 9:50.

3. *"Let your speech be alway with grace, seasoned with salt"*: A believer's *conversation* with others *"to answer every man"* should contain the *preserved* Words of Scripture. How is one to know how to truly answer another without the preserved words of God, as "there is no wisdom nor understanding nor counsel against the Lord," (Prov. 21:30)? No one can effectively answer any man without those preserved Words of God. "Salt" symbolically represents the pure and preserved words of God as will be confirmed by Scripture and by commentary from authors throughout the Church age. Psalm 12:6 reminds us that *"The words of the Lord are pure words: as silver tried in a furnace of earth, purified seven times."*[50] Notice the number seven used in verse 6 of Psalm 12 denotes perfection or completeness in God's economy.

4. *"That ye may know how ye ought to answer every man."*: A believer's *answers* contain God's words given with "grace." One cannot literally throw salt on our words as they come out of our mouths. Therefore, Paul was obviously referring to another (heteros) figurative or metaphorical aspect of salt. We are to season our speech with "salt," the Words of Scripture. Without a doubt, it is the grace of God that allows us to recall His Words during those critical times when they are so important.

---

[50] Thomas M. Strouse, "Essay, Psalm 12: 6-7 and the Permanent Preservation of God's Words" (*The Dean Burgon Society Messages From The 24th Annual Meeting. #12 in a Series,* Bible For Today, Collingswood, N.J.) p. 136-141. Please note that the correct translation of this verse is not found in the modern critical versions. A complete discussion of the exegesis and translation of Psalm 12:6-7 may be found in the article above.

CHAPTER 9

TWO IMPORTANT PASSAGES

Jesus also made metaphorical use of the word salt. This author believes the full or plenary understanding of His Words in several passages has been overlooked. Perhaps, this is the time for us to understand and apply a consistent interpretation of the word, salt, throughout Scripture.

The great debate over the issues raised by the modernistic disciplines of higher and lower textual criticism[51] has caused many individuals to closely reevaluate the Words of the Bible. Many have had their confidence shaken as a result. Others have questioned their sufficient application to personal situations. Some have overcome the adverse effects of all the theorizing by modern textual critics, but many have continued to doubt the preservation of the Words of God because of all the theories that have been raised. They have been answered, but most have not received or heard the facts concerning preservation of the Hebrew, Aramaic, and Greek Words.

In 2002, at an Annual Meeting of the Dean Burgon Society (DBS), this author was struck with the thought that so important an issue as the preservation of the Words of God *must be* covered or under-written also by a covenant in Scripture. God is a covenant-making God. The next year was spent investigating this "thought" as time would allow.

Gradually, the Covenant of Salt and the use of salt in the Scripture made more sense in light of the passages pertaining to these

---

[51] **Textual criticism** (or **lower criticism**) is a branch of literary criticism that is concerned with the identification and removal of transcription errors in the texts of manuscripts. **Historical criticism** or **higher criticism** is a branch of literary analysis that investigates the origins of a text: as applied in biblical studies it investigates the books of the Bible and compares them to other texts written at the same time, before, or recently after the text in question.

considerations. Previously, when researching this particular covenant, prior commentary by others had created a mental set that would not allow the full plenary meaning of the Covenant of Salt to be appreciated. Finally, each passage was inductively studied.

Interestingly, this author believes Jesus' comments clarify this issue in two important passages. In addition, Paul, the Hebrew of Hebrews who had studied under Gamaliel and knew the Old Testament better than most, presented a passage under guidance from the Holy Spirit that illuminated the use of salt as a metaphor. Hopefully this presentation will lead you to the same conclusions as this author.

Passage 1

In the Sermon on the Mount, Matthew 5-7, Jesus' comments were made *"when he was set, [and] his disciples came unto him"* (Mat. 5:1) His teachings were a 'millennium' beyond previous understanding of the Scripture. His comments will have great application for Israel during the millennial age when Israel is granted the title deed to all the land as the unconditional covenants guarantee. During the discourse, He said:

> *"Ye are the salt of the earth: but if the salt have lost his savour, wherewith shall it be salted? it is thenceforth good for nothing, but to be cast out, and to be trodden under foot of men." [Mat 5:13]*

How Can Man Be the Salt of the Earth?

Jesus was talking to his disciples who were believers. Yet, we know from Scripture that:

> *"The heart is deceitful above all things, and desperately wicked: who can know it?" [Jer. 17:9] "For all have sinned, and come short of the glory of God;"*

[Romans 3:23] ",... for the imagination of man's heart is evil from his youth;" [Genesis 8:21c].

How can man be the *salt* of the earth? Certainly it appears that Jesus was referring to 'true' believers who had the preserved, pure engrafted words of God in their heart (Psa. 37:31, 119:11, Isa 59:21, Pro. 30:5).[52] Jesus said *"Ye are the salt."* If the *salt* has become corrupted, or has *"lost his savour"*, or has changed, or has been added to or subtracted from, it is no longer useful, *"but to be cast out."*[53] It is the pure unadulterated, uncorrupted, preserved, pure Words of God in Hebrew, Aramaic and Greek (the *"foundation"*) accurately and faithfully translated into the languages of the world that empowers believers to be *"salt" (Heb. 4:12).*[54] By grace through faith they become salt by virtue of the indwelling of the Holy Spirit (Eph. 2:8-9) and His faithfully translated Words hid in a believer's heart. Faith comes by the Word(s) of God (Rom. 10:17). The Holy Spirit glorifies the Lord Jesus Christ and His Words, not Himself (Jn. 16:13). The preacher's preacher, Charles Haddon Spurgeon said:

> "I looked on Christ and the dove of peace flew into my heart; I looked on the dove of peace—and it flew away."

The preceding thoughts encompass the plan of the Trinity. The Scripture is clear that the three persons of the Trinity participate. The Spirit guided the apostles into the completion of the canon of Scripture:

> *But the Comforter, which is the Holy Ghost, whom the Father will send in my name, he shall teach you all*

---

[52] The permanent indwelling Spirit in believers did not come until Pentecost.

[53] The Scripture is clear that a corrupted believer or His Words corrupted are no longer useful.

[54] This is no different than accurate and faithful translations being quick, powerful, sharp, and a discerner of the thoughts and intents of the heart (Heb. 4:12).

*things, and bring all things to your remembrance, whatsoever **I have said** unto you. [John 14:26] But when the Comforter is come, whom I will send unto you from the Father, even the Spirit of truth, which proceedeth from the Father, he shall testify of me: [John 15.26] Howbeit when he, the Spirit of truth, is come, he will guide you into **all truth**: **for he shall not speak of himself**; but whatsoever **he shall hear**, that shall he speak: and he will shew you things to come. [John 16.13]*

"*All truth*" is the "*book of remembrance*" spoken of by Malachi (Mal. 3:16) and the "*remembrance*" of the prophets and apostles. The Apostle Peter spoke about it in his last will and testament[55] (2 Pe 3:1-2). It was mentioned by the Apostle Paul in his last written words (2 Tim 2:14-15). John said in his Gospel, "*thy Word is truth*" (Jn. 17:17). In the Church Age, the Holy Spirit, who is also called the Spirit of Truth, is within us and speaks "*whatsoever I [Jesus] shall say*" and "*whatsoever he shall hear*" from Jesus Christ (John 14:26). All of these things have application to "salt" and understanding it figurative use.

Passage 2

Following Jesus' comments on "*salt,*" the very next verse in Matthew 5 reveals Him commenting on "*light,*" which extends for the next 3 verses.

*"Ye are the **light** of the world. A city that is set on a hill cannot be hid. (15) Neither do men light a candle, and put it under a bushel, but on a candlestick; and it giveth **light** unto all that are in the house. (16) Let your **light** so shine before men, that they may see your good works, and glorify your Father which is in*

---

[55] Second Peter is the last Words recorded by Peter before his death and is therefore called his last will and testament. Similarly, 2 Timothy is Paul's last will and testament before his death.

heaven." [Matthew 5:14-16]

Man cannot be "the *light"* without the preserved Words of God, accurately and faithfully translated, and engrafted into a man's heart. Man is desperately wicked (Jer. 17:9). However, the Words of God are *light*. Psalm 119:130 says:

"The entrance of thy words giveth light; it giveth understanding unto the simple."

and Psalm 105 says:

"Thy word is a lamp unto my feet, and a light unto my path."

Furthermore, Isaiah said that if one does not declare or *"speak according to this word,"* the Scripture, there is no light in him. Someone cannot adequately 'speak' the Scripture without quoting it.

To the law and to the testimony: if they speak not according to this word, it is because there is no light in them. [Isaiah 8:20]

Therefore, *"Ye are salt"* and *"Ye are light,"* by virtue of the preserved Words of God in your heart, symbolically represented by *"salt."*

The "Salt" Is From One Shepherd

In Ecclesiastes, Solomon says

*"The words of the wise are as goads, and as nails fastened by the masters of assemblies, which are **given from one shepherd."** [Ecc 12:11]*

Interestingly, after Jesus presents His thoughts on *"salt"* and *"light,"* He immediately launches into the next idea concerning the complete, absolute preservation of the Scripture with the following declaration in Mat 5:17-18:

> *"Think not that I am come to destroy the law, or the prophets: I am not come to destroy, but to fulfil. 18 For verily I say unto you, Till heaven and earth pass, one jot or one tittle shall in no wise pass from the law, till all be fulfilled."*

Jesus did not come to remove, change, subtract, or add to the Old Testament Scripture, and to "top it all off," He said the smallest part would not be lost (Mat. 5:17-18). He came to fulfill Scripture to the "jot and tittle."

Also, we know that during His incarnation, He also gave us more Words from the Father (Jn 14:24, 17:14). Preceding Mat 5:17-18, Jesus made it abundantly clear that only believers would understand the importance of His judgments. Why? Because they are the *"salt"* and the *"light"* by virtue of the preserved Words in their heart, which were recorded in Heaven and given by Jesus to man to record through the agency of the Holy Spirit. They are translated by commandment into the languages of the world (Rom 16:26). The *salt* is the preserved Words of God engrafted into the heart of the believer so that he is able to be the light and salt of the world. Jesus indicated that not one letter of the pure, inerrant, infallible preserved *"Salt"* in Hebrew, Aramaic and Greek would be lost. It would be the foundation for translations. According to Paul, our speech is to be *"seasoned"* with the *"salt"* of God.

> *Let your speech be alway with grace, seasoned with salt, that ye may know how ye ought to answer every man. Colossians 4:6*

CHAPTER 10

THE ETERNAL COVENANT

The Salt of the Covenant

The Covenant of Salt, presented in the Old Testament, takes on renewed meaning in light of the New Testament pronouncements of Jesus and Paul. The Covenant of Salt was not fully explained in the Old Testament, just as other concepts were not fully explained. Therefore, 'the Old Testament is the New Testament concealed, and the New Testament is the Old Testament revealed.'

This author believes the plenary, hermeneutical application of the Covenant in the Church age was planned *"for such a time such as this"* when God's Words continue to be corrupted by unbelief and a false Bibliology.

> *"And every oblation of thy meat offering shalt thou season with salt; neither shalt thou suffer **the salt of the covenant of thy God ["salt", symbolically** representing **the Words of God, and "the covenant", Jesus Christ]** to be lacking from thy meat offering: with **all** thine offerings thou shalt offer <u>salt</u>." [Lev. 2: 13] [my addition and emphasis, HDW]*

Please take notice of the way *"the salt of the covenant"* is phrased: **the** salt of **the** covenant. It is not "a" covenant. The *"salt"* is the Words of *"the covenant;"* the Covenant is the Lord Jesus Christ. This will be more fully developed below.

God made it perfectly clear that *"with **all** thine offerings"* salt was to be offered. This included the burnt offering, the meal offering, the peace offering, the sin offering, the trespass offering, the wave offering, the drink offering, the heave offering, the shewbread, and *"all"* the offerings (Leviticus 2:13). Why did God command this; why was it needed; and what does it symbolically represent?

There is great symbolism or typology in the sacrifices and the Tabernacle of Moses in the Old Testament pertaining to the Lord Jesus Christ. Most believers recognize the Old Testament is about Jesus Christ, The Word (John 1:1ff). Most authors recognize that the Covenant of Salt represents a quote, unquote "eternal covenant," but no comment is made related to its typology. Although many authors do comment on the hermeneutics or interpretation as related to:

(1) faithfulness,

(2) friendship,

(3) purity,

(4) loyalty,

(5) eternality,

(6) permanency, or

(7) indissolubleness,

most do not apply one consistent meaning throughout Scripture.

Some suggestions for the reason God commanded "salt" offered with "every" sacrifice are:

(1) the recognition that the Words of Scripture are a *"covenant for ever"* (Psa. 105:8), represented by "salt," which will judge us (Jn. 12:47-48); and

(2) the understanding that Jesus is also the *"everlasting covenant"* represented by "salt" (q.v.) (Gen. 17:7, Mal. 3:1, Gal 3:17).

> *And I will establish **my covenant** between me and thee and thy seed after thee in their generations for **an everlasting covenant, to be a God unto thee**, and to thy seed after thee. Genesis 17:7*

(3) Salt is a preservative, just as the Words of God preserve (keep) us for heaven (eternity).

Jesus is the Messenger of the Covenant
and the Covenant Itself

In Genesis 17:7, *"my covenant"* literally means the Abrahamic Covenant. However, hermeneutically, the Scripture frequently contains a second, third, or even fourth spiritual meaning. The Lord Jesus Christ is our *"covenant,"* our *"everlasting covenant,"* our *"God,"* our *Saviour,"* etc. The Bible is all about the Lord Jesus Christ. These concepts are emphasized throughout the Bible. He is the Covenant and the Messenger of the Covenant. Here are the some of the verses.

In Isaiah 42:6-7, 49:8, the context reveals that God assigns the title, Covenant, to the Lord Jesus Christ, and Jesus' quotes Isaiah 61:2, in the New Testament, which has reference to Isaiah 42:7 also, as referring to him:

> *I the LORD have called thee in righteousness, and will hold thine hand, and will keep thee, and give **thee** for a **covenant** of the people, for a light of the Gentiles; To open the blind eyes, to bring out the prisoners from the prison, and them that sit in darkness out of the prison house. Isaiah 42:6-7*

> *Thus saith the LORD, In an acceptable time have I heard thee, and in a day of salvation have I helped thee: and I will preserve thee, and give **thee** for a **covenant** of the people, to establish the earth, to cause to inherit the desolate heritages; Isaiah 49:8*

Exegetically, the verses have reference to Him (e.g. Isa. 42:6-7, theologically parallels Isa. 61:1-2). The following verses were quoted by Jesus as applying to Him.

> *The Spirit of the Lord GOD is upon me; because the LORD hath anointed me to preach good tidings unto the meek; he hath sent me to bind up the brokenhearted, to proclaim liberty to the captives, and the opening of the prison to them that are bound;To*

proclaim the acceptable year of the LORD, and the day of vengeance of our God; to comfort all that mourn; Isaiah 61:1-2 (In Lk. 4:18, Jesus leaves off the end of Isa. 61:2 because that applies to the second part of His second coming, HDW)

Behold, I will send my messenger, and he shall prepare the way before me: and the Lord, whom ye seek, shall suddenly come to his temple, even the **messenger of the covenant**, *whom ye delight in: behold, he shall come, saith the LORD of hosts. Malachi 3:1*

Logically,

If: The Covenant = the Lord Jesus Christ (Isa. 42:6) &

        The Covenant = the Words of God (Old and New Testament) &

        Salt   = the Words of God (Old and New Testament)

Then: Salt   = the Lord Jesus Christ

Salt is the type of the antitype, Jesus Christ **or** the pure, preserved Words of God. Jesus, The Word, is the one who was totally consumed and totally "burnt" on the altar of sacrifice as salt for us. In addition, the preserved Words are to judge all our sacrifices. [John 12:47-48]

The Word of God is salt; and all of our sacrifices, all of our speech, all of our conversation, and all of our conduct are to be "salted." If they are not, then they lose their *"sweet savour" (Lev. 2:12-13)*

Leviticus 2:12-13 "As for the oblation of the firstfruits, ye shall offer them unto the LORD: but they shall not be burnt on the altar for a **sweet savour**. *And every oblation of thy meat offering shalt thou season with* **salt**; *neither shalt thou suffer* **the salt of the covenant of thy God to be lacking** *from thy meat offering: with all thine offerings thou shalt offer salt.*

We are not to live by bread alone, but by **every word** from God, which adds *"sweet savour"* to our lives. [Mat. 4:4, Deut. 8:3]. He is the

Bread; He is the Salt; He is the Word; He is the Eternal Covenant; He is the Savour who redeemed us to eternal life.

Everything we do, think, and say is to have Him and His words included. We are to be bathed in "Salt" as a newborn babe because it purifies (Eze 16:4, Eph. 5:25-27). In the days of Jerusalem's nativity and pollution, "the Lord GOD" said that the city was not "salted."

> Ezekiel 16:4 *"And as for thy nativity, in the day thou wast born thy navel was not cut, neither wast thou washed in water to supple thee; thou wast not **salted** at all, nor swaddled at all."* (my emphasis, HDW)

The Words of Jesus wash and cleanse us (Eph. 5:26). When our children are not washed in the *"living water"* and *"salted,"* they often go astray. Jesus and His Words are our first love because they are pure, preserved, and eternal; they are from God; they are our Salvation in the Lord Jesus Christ; and they are a sure foundation. They are our 'salt' by which we are to be "salted."

*Ezekiel 16:4 "And as for thy nativity, in the day thou wast born thy navel was not cut, neither wast thou washed in water to supple thee; thou wast not **salted** at all, nor swaddled at all."*

*Ezra 6:9 "And that which they have need of, both young bullocks, and rams, and lambs, for the burnt offerings of the God of heaven, wheat, **salt**, wine, and oil, according to the appointment of the priests which are at Jerusalem, let it be given them day by day without fail:"*

CHAPTER 11

DIFFICULT TO UNDERSTAND PASSAGES

Mark 9:49-50

The following passage is another one that many authors report as difficult to understand. Jesus said in Mark 9:49-50:

> *"For **everyone** shall be salted with fire, and every sacrifice shall be salted with salt. Salt is good: but if the salt have lost his saltness, wherewith will ye season it? Have salt in yourselves, and have peace one with another."*

Without the proper understanding of the meaning of salt, the passage in Mark nine seems obscure. Matthew Henry states:

> "The two last verses (He is referring to Mark 9:49-50, HDW) are **somewhat difficult,** and interpreters agree not in the sense of them,; [sic] for every one in general, or rather every one of them that are cast into hell, shall be *salted with fire, and every sacrifice shall be salted with salt.* Therefore have *salt in yourselves.* It was appointed by the law of Moses, that every sacrifice should be *salted with salt*, not to preserve it (for it was to be immediately consumed), but because it was the fold of God's table, and no flesh is eaten without salt; it was therefore particularly required in the meat offerings."[56] [my emphasis, HDW]

[56] *Matthew Henry's Commentary on the Whole Bible: New Modem Edition Database,* Hendrickson's Publishers, Inc., AGES Software Albany, or; Version 1.0; p. 1151-1153.

Albert Barnes writes is his commentary, *Barnes Notes*, the following concerning the difficulty of the verses.

> Mark 9:49 "Every one shall be salted with fire": <u>Perhaps no passage in the New Testament has given more perplexity to commentators than this</u>, and it may be impossible now to fix its precise meaning. The common idea affixed to it has been, that as salt preserves from putrefaction, so fire, applied to the wicked in hell, will have the property of preserving them in existence, or they will "be" preserved amid the sprinkling of fire, to be continually in their sufferings a sacrifice to the justice of God; but this meaning is not quite satisfactory. Another opinion has been, that as salt was sprinkled on the victim preparatory to its being devoted to God (see <u>Lev 2:13)</u>, so would "the apostles," by trials, calamities, etc., represented here by "fire," be prepared as a sacrifice and offering to God. Probably the passage has no reference at all to future punishment; and the difficulty of interpreting it has arisen from supposing it to be connected with the 48th verse, or given as a "reason" for what is said in "that" verse, rather than considering it as designed to illustrate the "general design" of the passage. The main scope of the passage was not to discourse of future punishment; that is brought in incidentally. The chief object of the passage was -
> 1. To teach the apostles that "other men," not "with them," might be true Christians, <u>Mar 9:38-39.</u>
> 2. That they ought to be disposed to look favorably upon the slightest evidence that they "might be true believers," <u>Mar 9:41.</u>
> 3. That they ought to avoid giving "offence" to such feeble and obscure Christians, <u>Mar 9:42</u>.
> 4. That "everything" calculated to give offence, or to dishonor religion, should be removed, <u>Mar 9:43</u>. And,
> 5. That everything which would endanger their salvation should be sacrificed; that they should "deny" themselves in every way in order to obtain eternal life. In this way they would be "preserved" to eternal life.
> **The word "fire," here, therefore denotes self-denials,** sacrifices, trials, in keeping ourselves from

> the gratification of the flesh. As if he had said, "Look at the sacrifice on the altar. It is an offering to God, about to be presented to him. It is sprinkled with "salt, emblematic of purity, of preservation and of fitting it, therefore, for a sacrifice." So "you" are devoted to God. You are sacrifices, victims, offerings to him in his service. To make you "acceptable" offerings, every thing must be done to "preserve" you from sin and to "purify" you. Self-denials, subduing the lusts, enduring trials, removing offences, are the proper "preservatives" in the service of God. Doing this, you will be acceptable offerings and be saved; without this, you will be "unfit" for his eternal service and will be lost."[57] [my emphasis]

This author does not believe the word "fire" denotes "self-denials." The probable meaning is that the preserved, pure words of God will judge **everyone** and every idle word [Mat. 12:36]; they will judge every sacrifice or deed; they are *"like a fire"* (Jer. 23:29, see below). To be judged by God's Words is to be "salted" by His Words. Can anyone deny the discomfort and severe pain "like a fire" if salt is poured into a wound?

Mark 9:49-50 **are** difficult to understand **without** the definition of "salt" as the pure, preserved, eternal words of Scripture or as the Covenant of God, Jesus Christ (Gal. 3:17). Three additional Scriptures support this exegesis of Mark 9:49. John 12:47-50 says:

> *"And if any man hear my words, and believe not, I judge him not: for I came not to judge the world, but to save the world. 48He that rejecteth me, and receiveth not **my words,** hath one that judgeth him: the word that I have spoken, the same shall **judge** him in the last day. 49For I have not spoken of myself; but the Father which sent me, he gave me a commandment, what I should say, and what I should speak. 50And I know that his commandment is life everlasting: whatsoever I speak therefore, even as the Father said*

---

[57] Barnes, Albert, Notes on the Bible, E-sword 7.05 Electronic Edition; Rick Meyers Trademark; www.e- sword.net.

unto me, so I speak.

Luke records that Jesus said,

"I am come to send fire on the earth; and what will I if it be already kindled?" Luke 12:49

The Word of God is like a fire. Jeremiah 23:29 says,

"Is not my word like as a fire? saith the Lord; and like a hammer that breaketh the rock in pieces?"

Therefore, *"everyone will be salted with fire"* or everyone will be judged with the word which is *"like as a fire"* [and] *"like a hammer"* [Jer. 23:29]. Everyone's "sacrifice"[58] shall be judged with Salt, which are the preserved, pure Words of Scripture. Mark 9:49-50 should now make more sense with this understanding of the meaning of *"salt."*

Salt was to be added to every sacrifice because salt stood for the pure preserved words of God that would judge every sacrifice and will "in the last day" judge every one of us. The Words of God are to be added to our speech, and it is to be our daily bread. It gives eternal life and is our light. Salt, the preserved, pure words, is the Eternal Covenant (Num. 18:9). The Salt is a preserver and sustainer. The Salt of God will never lose its "savour" unless it is added to, corrupted, changed, subtracted from or otherwise manipulated by man. Therefore Jesus added the words of Mark 9:50:

*Salt is good: but if the salt have lost his saltness, wherewith will ye season it? Have **salt in yourselves,** and have peace one with another.*

Peace will never come to this world until the "Salt" rules *"with a rod of iron"* (Rev 19:15.

---

[58] In the Church Age 'sacrifice' should be understood as referring to the work of the saints, to the committing our bodies to the service of the Lord, and to our bodies as the temple of God (Rom 12:1-2, 1 Cor. 3:17, 6:19, 2 Cor. 6:16).

CHAPTER 12

CORRUPTING THE WORDS
OF GOD IS FORBIDDEN

God is Watching Those Who Corrupt

The travesty of *believers* manipulating God's Words in these "last days" was also addressed in the Sermon on the Mount. Jesus said,

> *Whosoever therefore shall **break** one of these least commandments, and shall **teach** men so, he shall be called the least in the kingdom of heaven: but whosoever shall **do** and **teach** them, the same shall be called great in the kingdom of heaven. For I say unto you, That except your righteousness shall exceed the righteousness of the scribes and Pharisees, ye shall in no case enter into the kingdom of heaven. Matthew 5:19-20* [59]

Jesus was not only addressing obedience to these commandments, but he was also specifically addressing the loosing, destroying, corrupting or breaking the literal Words of the commandments He had just given. They are His Words. If someone has read through and understands the Bible, he would know the great significance and importance God places upon His Words.

In the context of the passage in question (Mat. 5:13-20), He was not using parallelism in this passage. In other words, "break" has nothing to do with "do" in the same verse. In the first instance, He used a Greek work which means to corrupt. He was addressing those who

---

[59] This author understands the Jewish hermeneutics of the Sermon on the Mount, but also understands the homiletic application of the verses.

would "break,"[60] destroy, dissolve, corrupt, change, add to, or subtract from His Words. Therefore, those who practice "luo" (Greek for break) of His Words, or free others from His Words by altering or adjusting their intended meaning in any way shall be called "least."

In addition, it is very likely that Jesus was pointing out that the Jew's oral law, later called the Mishna when it was recorded, was a construction of man, and was "luo" and not from the heart. It was legalistic (Mat. 23). Jesus was proclaiming that the type of ideas, tradition, or constructions of man reflected in the Jewish oral law were far short of the needed understanding and application of the pure and preserved words of Scripture. It is a matter of the heart, not of legalistic rules established *"for to be seen of men"* (Mat. 23:5). The kind of human reasoning that led to the oral law of the Pharisees is what Jesus was indicating would lead to "breaking" [luo] His Words, which determine the commandments from God (Mat. 5:19-20). Destroying the Words of God in any way is forbidden. It is the very thing that modem textual critics and many translators do.[61] They break the "covenant."

The Covenant of God

As previously mentioned, Isaiah presents the Lord as a Covenant

---

[60] luo, Greek 3089, Strong's a primary verb; to *"loosen"* (literal or figurative):- break (up), destroy, dissolve, (un-) loose, melt, put off. Compare Greek 4486 (rhegnumi). rhegnumi, Greek 4486, Strong's or *rhesso,* hrace'-so; both prolonged forms of rheko (which appears only in certain forms, and is itself probably a strengthened form of agnumi [see in Greek 2608 (katagnumi)]); to *"break," "wreck"* or *"crack,"* i.e. (especially) to *sunder* (by *separation* of the parts; Greek 2608 (katagnumi) being its intensive [with the preposition in comparative], and Greek 2352 (thrauo) a *shattering* to minute fragments; but not a *reduction* to the constituent particles, like Greek 3089 (luo» or *disrupt, lacerate;* by implication to *convulse* (with *spasms);* figurative to *give vent* to joyful emotions :- break (forth), burst, rend, tear.

[61] See this excellent work. Pastor D. A. Waite, Th.D., Ph.D., *Defending the King James Bible,* (The Bible For Today Press, Collingswood, NJ).

in several passages. He is also presented by Isaiah as the "light" (Jn. 9:5), as being preserved, and as the preserver. **Isaiah 42:6** says

> *"I the Lord have called thee in righteousness, and will hold thine hand, and will **keep** thee, and give thee for a **covenant** of the people, for a **light** of the Gentiles;"*

Isaiah 49:8 says,

> *"Thus saith the Lord, In an acceptable time have I heard thee, and in a day of salvation have I helped thee: and I will **preserve** thee, and give thee for a **covenant** of the people, **to establish the earth, to cause to inherit the desolate heritages;"** [See Mal. 3:1 below]*

"Thee" in these verses is none other than the Captain of our souls. The Lord Jesus Christ would: (1) be the preserver of the earth, (2) be a (preserved) covenant, and (3) be Himself preserved. "Salt" preserves and gives life. We cannot live without salt. Salt is composed of sodium and chloride (NaCl). It is the major cation[62] in the blood. When a doctor is treating a patient in the hospital with intravenous fluids, he must determine the level of salt (Na and Cl) in the blood. If it is not correct, the patient may die.

The Lord Jesus Christ's Words are the Words of life just as He is **the** Word of life. Man cannot live without the Word or the Words (Jn. 3:15-16, Mat. 4:4). Typologically, they are the salt (sodium and chloride, NaCl in our blood). "The life of the flesh is in the blood" (Lev. 17:11).

The Lord Jesus Christ is *"**the** covenant."* (Lev 2:13) *"to establish the earth"* (Isa 49:8). He is the Creator (Eph. 3:9), Sustainer (Heb. 1:3), and Judge (Jn. 12:47-48). It is His preserving Words that should be

---

[62] "An ion or group of ions having a positive charge and characteristically moving toward the negative electrode in electrolysis." (from the Free Dictionary)

adhered to or added to **"all"** that we do. They should 'season' our speech, be a light to our path, be our way, our understanding, our wisdom, our guide,........., (you add more).

What more can be said?!

CHAPTER 13

THE COVENANT

Jesus Christ is the *"Covenant"* (see above) and He is *"The Messenger of the Covenant."*

> Malachi 3:1 *"Behold, I will send my messenger, and he shall prepare the way before me: and the Lord, whom ye seek, shall suddenly come to his temple, even **the messenger of the covenant,** whom ye delight in: behold, he shall come, saith the Lord of hosts."*

Jesus is the *"Everlasting Covenant."* Genesis 17:7 says,

> *"And I will establish **my covenant** between me and thee and thy seed after thee in their generations for **<u>an everlasting covenant, to be a God</u>** unto thee, and to thy seed after thee"*

God's Covenant was to be *"everlasting"* and *"my covenant."* God was not only to be Abraham's God and the covenant was not only the Abrahamic Covenant, but God is also the "everlasting covenant." He is "the Lord Jesus Christ" as noted above and in Hebrews 13:20, which says:

> *"Now the God of peace, that brought again from the dead our Lord Jesus, that great shepherd of the sheep, through the blood of the **everlasting covenant**"*

*"The blood of the **everlasting covenant**"* is none other than the blood of Jesus Christ who is the *"everlasting covenant."*

> "And I will make an everlasting covenant with you - On

the word 'covenant,' see the notes at **Isa** 28:18; 42:6; 49:8. **Here it means that God would bind himself to be their God, their protector, and their friend.** This covenant would be made with all who would come to him. It would not be with the nation of the Jews, as such, or with any community, as such, but it would be with all who should embrace the offers of life and salvation."[63]

Galatians 3:17 says:

And this I say, that **the covenant**, that was confirmed before **of God in Christ,** the law, which was four hundred and thirty years after, cannot disannul, that it should make the promise of none effect.

"God in Christ" means Jesus Christ is God and He is the Covenant, which was confirmed in the Abrahamic Covenant 430 years before "the law." Also, we know that the Lamb was ordained from the foundation of the world (Rev. 13:8), but He was affirmed in the Abrahamic Covenant. He is the *"[B]lessing"* from *"Abram"* for *"all families of the earth"* (Gen. 12:1-3).

The Names of Jesus From Psalm 119

Jesus is the *Everlasting Covenant* that guarantees a believer's justification before God by His blood that was shed on the Cross for our sins. By the virtues of the Lord, His nature, and His Words, the following names can be garnered from Psa. 119: He is The Statutes, The Promise, The Judge, The Testimonies, The Way, The Precepts, The Law, The Truth, The Fear (of Isaac), The Mercy, Kindness, The Loving Kindness, The Lamp, The Surety, The Light, The Commandments, The Pure, The Dawning of the Morning, The Lord, The Word, The Wondrous Things, The Counseller, The Merciful, The Gracious, The

---

[63] Albert Barnes, *Notes on the Old Testament, Explanatory and Practical* (comments on Isa. 55:3).

Portion, The My Delight, The Faithfulness, The Honey, The Wonderful, The Surety, The Everlasting Righteousness, The Near, The Tender Mercies, The Righteous Judgments, The Praise of My Lips, The Salvation...

He is The Covenant of God, The Everlasting Covenant, and by virtue of His blood that provides everlasting redemption, The Redeemer is the Covenant.

Numbers 18:19 says

> *"by a **statute for ever: it is a covenant of salt for ever** before the Lord unto thee and to thy :seed with thee.*

Please note that "forever" is repeated twice to be certain the concept of "everlasting" is not missed. The Covenant of Salt is an Everlasting Covenant, which is a metaphor, and symbolically is Jesus and/or The Word(s). The Psalmist said, "He hath remembered **his covenant for ever, the word** which be commanded to a thousand generations" (Psalm 105:8)..

The passage dealing with salt cast into *"the spring of the waters"* at Jericho by Elisha should now be easy to understand. The great Purifier and agent of the Purifier, the Words of God, which washes and cleanses us cured the water (See 2 Kings 2:19-22). (The discussion of Lot's wife is below.)

Isaiah 55:11 "So shall my word be that goeth forth out of my mouth: it shall not return unto me void, but it shall accomplish that which I please, and it shall prosper in the thing whereto I sent it."

CHAPTER 14

COMMENTS ON THE COVENANT OF SALT BY OTHER AUTHORS

The review of many publications reveals that numerous authors came close to calling the Covenant of Salt representative of the preserved Words of God.

Comments by Dr. Timothy Cross

For example, Timothy Cross said that "salt" represents "covenant" and that Christ is the "salt." He said,

> [the] "Covenant concept is part of the very warp and woof of the Bible, which is divided into two, the Old Covenant and the New Covenant. The 'Covenant' refers to the binding bond which God lovingly makes between Himself and His people...Salt was a sign of God's covenant with His Old Testament people."[64] "Jesus said of His new covenant people: You are the salt of the earth (Matthew 5:13) and while it is not explicit, it is implicit that what is to be true of the Christian was actually true of the Christ."[65]

Without a doubt, Jesus is the Word; He is the salt. Therefore, Dr. Cross is implicitly saying Christians are the salt also, because they have the preserved engrafted Words of God in them and the Lord Jesus Christ, the Father, and the Holy Spirit indwelling (Jn. 14:17, 23).

---

[64] Timothy Cross, Ph.D., *Scent From Heaven*: (Ambassadors Productions, Limited; Providence House; Belfast); 1994; ISBN 0-907927-88-2; p.40.
[65] Ibid; p. 41.

> "Salt is a pure substance, and was used in Biblical times to purify...Salt thus speaks to us of the immaculate purity of Christ"[66] [and this author would add, the Scripture. HDW]

It is well known that salt was used in Old Testament times to purify the skin of babies (Eze. 16:4). Implicitly, salt represents the pure Words of God that purify (Psa. 12:6, 30:5, Eph. 5:26).

> "The sinless Christ was not subject to the law of death and decay"[67]

Why? Because THE sinless Christ and His Words are the salt which cleanses and prevents decay. Without consuming "salt," a person would literally perish (die). Salt is necessary for our actual existence in the flesh. Similarly, without the typological meaning of salt, man perishes also:

> "But he answered and said, It is written, Man shall not live by bread alone, but by every word that proceedeth out of the mouth of God." Matthew 4:4

> "And I give unto them eternal life; and they shall never perish, neither shall any man pluck them out of my hand." John 10:28

Without Jesus a person will perish eternally. Without God's Words a person will perish eternally (Psa 1:6, 2:12, 73:27, 119:92, Lk. 13:3, Jn. 3:15-16, 10:28). He is the Resurrection and the Life by virtue of being the Living Word (John 11 :25).

Salt is a substance that creates great thirst and we are drawn to water. Similarly, the Words of God and the Lord Jesus Christ, which are typologically salt, draw us to the "living water" (Jn. 4:10). Dr. Cross said:

---

[66] Ibid; p. 41.
[67] Ibid; p.42.

"Before we come to Christ, God may see fit to give us a raging spiritual thirst."[68]

This is the thirst that can only be quenched by the Living Word.

Comments by Dr. A. R. Fausset

However, the engrafted pure "salt" continues to make one thirsty for the Living Water. A.R. Fausset comments on Mark 9:49-50 discussed above:

"It signifies the imperishableness of Jehovah's love for his people,; as an antiseptic salt implies durability, fidelity, purity. **The opposite of leaven, the symbol of corruption**. [sic] Covenants were cemented by feasts and hospitality, the viands of which were seasoned, as all foods, with salt. Hence, "a covenant of salt for ever before the Lord" is an indissoluble covenant."[69]

He is right. The Covenant of Salt is indissoluble because it is the preserved words of God, settled in heaven and given to us by Jesus and the Holy Ghost. "[T]he Scripture cannot be broken" (Jn. 10:35). The "corrupted" words of God found in such publications as the *NIV*, Living Bible, The Message," etc., does have leaven in them. Although they contain the Words of God, many passages have Words missing because the translations were based upon the wrong original texts. Modern versions are "broken." A. R. Fausset goes on to say that Colossians 4:6 means:

"let your speech be always with grace, seasoned with

---

[68] Ibid; p.43.
[69] *Fausset's Bible Dictionary*, NAAM-ZUZIMS by A.R. Fausset, To the Students of the Words, Works and Ways of God; AGES Digital Library; Albany, OR; p. 467-468.

salt", i.e. the savour of fresh spiritual wisdom excluding all "corrupt communication", and tasteless unpro-fitableness or insipidty.[70]

Paul meant more than "fresh spiritual wisdom." He meant for our "speech" to contain the Words of God. If that is what Dr. Fausset meant, he is correct.

A Comment by John Wesley

The comments by many authors, whose theology was either Calvinistic or Armenian, showed a distinct bias for salt being representative of grace. John Wesley comments that after God places the law in the minds and the Spirit in the heart of the people of Israel:

> All their "conversation will be seasoned with salt," and will "minister grace to the hearers;" seeing it will not be so much they that speak, "as the Spirit of their Father that speaketh in them."[71]

This good comment is typical of the comments on salt by John Wesley.

Comments by John Bunyan

John Bunyan's editor as well as Bunyan himself thought salt was "faith" which cured the bitter waters of Elisha's miracle in 2 Kings 2:19-22,

> **Faith,** in the heart of a Christian, **is like the salt** that was thrown into the corrupt fountain, that made the

---

[70] Ibid; p.467-468.
[71] Works of John Wesley, Ages Software, Version 1.0, Albany, OR, 1997, Vol 6, Sermon 63, Isaiah 11:9, p. 305.

naughty waters good, and the barren land fruitful[72]

"So then faith *cometh* by hearing, and hearing by the word of God" (Romans 10:17), but it is the Words of God that give a man faith, which leads to the Holy Spirit's regeneration, indwelling, baptism (of the Spirit), and sealing of a man.

Bunyan also called salt the "grace of fear,"

> "Therefore this **grace of fear** is that without which no part or piece of service which we do to God, can be accepted of him. It is, as I may call it, "**the salt of the covenant,**"[73]

Bunyan also called someone unsanctified who had not been washed or salted. His description came upon the heels of reviewing God's account of cleansing the nation Israel (Eze. 16:8-9). His description speaks of the functions of the Words of God and the Holy Spirit to sanctify a nation or individual.

> I say, while they are unwashed, unswaddled, *unsalted*, but bloody sinners; for by these words, "not washed, not *salted*, not swaddled," he setteth forth their *unsanctified* state; yea, they were not only *unsanctified*, but also cast out, without pity, to the loathing of their persons;[74]

Although Bunyan does not call salt a type of the antitype, Scripture (the Words of God), he does everything but that in this section in his work.

Understanding Lot's Wife as a Pillar of Salt

---

[72] Bunyan's Practical Works; Ages Software, Version 1.0, Albany, OR, Vol 4, *Editors Advertisement,* p. 10, *A Holy Life*, p. 67.
[73] Ibid; *Fear of God,* Vol , p. 204.
[74] Ibid; Vol. 7; *Justification By Imputed Righteousness* p. 104.

A great number of comments are made in the works sighted concerning Lot's wife becoming *"a pillar of salt"* (Gen. 19:26). All of them concentrate on the disobedience of his wife. Perhaps some consideration should be given to the following:

1. A pillar is a witness in most places where it is used in the Scripture.

2. If one agrees that salt represents the pure preserved Words of Scripture, then the essence of the typology of a "pillar of salt" is this: The pillar is a witness to the truth of God's Words. Lot's wife was commanded to *"not look behind thee."* [Gen 19:19] The result was judgment by 'the Word(s)' and she became a witness to *"the truth of God,"* as a pillar of salt. God's Word(s) is Truth (Jn. 17:17).

Comments by John Calvin

John Calvin comes close to calling "salt" the Words of God in the following passage. Notice he places the responsibility of representatives of God to "not speak their own pleasure, but faithfully deliver the commands of him by whom they are sent" and to be "subject to the word of the Lord."

> Now, if you look to the apostles, they are commended by many distinguished titles, as the Light of the world, and **the Salt** of the earth, to be heard in Christ's stead, whatever they bound or loosed on earth being bound or loosed in heaven [Matthew 5:13, 14; Luke 10:16; John 20:23]. But they declare in their own name what the authority was which their office conferred on them -viz. if they are apostles they must not speak their own pleasure, but faithfully deliver **the commands** of him by whom they are sent. The words in which Christ defined their embassy are sufficiently clear, "Go ye, therefore, and teach all nations, teaching them to observe all things whatsoever I have commanded you" [Matthew 28:19, 20]. Nay, that none might be permitted to decline this law, he received it and imposed it on himself. "My doctrine is not mine, but his

that sent me" [John 7: 16]. He who always was the only and eternal counsellor of the Father, who by the Father was constituted Lord and Master of all, yet because he performed the ministry of teaching, prescribed to, all ministers by his example the rule which they ought to follow in teaching. The power of the Church, therefore, is not infinite, but is subject to **the word of the Lord**, and, as it were, included in it.[75] [my emphasis]

Finally, Calvin does address salt as "the Word of God" in his *Institutes of the Christian Religion.*

Their unction, therefore, is without savor; it wants **salt**, that is, **the word of God**.76

A Comment by Dr. Charles G. Finney

Charles G. Finney calls salt the gospel and presumably therefore the Word of God.

When abroad among strangers, I often ask individuals, "Do you not know of some one or more within your personal acquaintance, who really honor **the gospel**?" Some, perhaps, will answer, no; but if you converse with them much, you are likely to conclude that they are either dishonest or untruthful. For with most remarkable forethought, God, in His providence, has **scattered some salt all abroad over Christian lands,** so that every man shall have the moral trial of deciding whether he will or will not receive the lessons which **it** teaches.[77] [my emphasis]

---

[75] John Calvin, *Institutes of the Christian Religion:* Ages Software, Albany, OR; Version 1.0, Book 4, p. 1181.
[76] Ibid, p. 1482.
[77] Charles G. Finney, *The Finney Sermon Collection Vol. 1-3,* AGES Software, Albany, OR, Version 1.0, Vol II; p. 105.

A Comment by Martin Luther

Martin Luther's comments on the Sermon on the Mount seems to suggest that salt is the word of God, although he does not express it directly. There are no occurrences of "salt" in *The 95 Theses*.

> Christ, in Matthew 5-7, teaches briefly these points: first, as to the eight happinesses or blessings, how every Christian ought particularly to live as it concerns himself; secondly, of the office of teaching, what and how a man ought to teach in the church, how to season with **salt** and enlighten, reprove, and comfort, and exercise the faith; thirdly, he confutes and opposes the false expounding of the law; fourthly, he condemns the wicked hypocritical kind of living; fifthly, he teaches what are upright and good works; sixthly, he warns men of false doctrine; seventhly, he clears and solves what might be found doubtful and confused; eighthly, he condemns the hypocrites and false saints, who abuse **the precious word of grace**.[78] [my emphasis]

Comments By Others

Many of the works of D. L. Moody, William Law, John Owen, Jonathan Edwards, Basil (the Bishop of Caesarea), Gregory of Nizianzen, Ambrose, Sulpitus Serverus, Leo the Great, and Tertullian were examined and no comment on salt applicable to the subject at hand could be found.

Some of Arthur Pink's writings were examined. He reports that salt is the apostles, prophets, ministers, and that the word is savory salt. He reports appropriately that "If the word be mixed with dust and rubbish it loses its pungency and efficacy."

---

[78] Martin Luther, *Table Talk* AGES Software, Version 1.0, Albany, OR; p. 13.

A Comment by C. H. Spurgeon

C. H. Spurgeon consistently referred to "salt" as grace, or the remnant (believers) as salt. His comments are typified by the following:

> "There has always been a **salt of grace** in the world to counteract the power of sin."[79] "there is "a **remnant** according to the election of grace;" there is "**salt**," **[a remnant]** and for the sake of that **salt [grace]**, many who have defiled their garments **in** a measure will be saved."[80] [my additions in brackets for clarity and my emphasis]

A Comment by Ignatius

In the *Epistle of Ignatius to the Ephesians,* Ignatius implies a plant that is "bitter and salt" is of the devil, but in another place he implies "salt" is the sustainer and purifier, Jesus Christ.

> *"Take heed that no plant of the devil be found among you, for such a plant is bitter and salt. "Watch ye, and be ye sober," in Christ Jesus.*[81] *"Be ye salted in Him, lest any one among you should be corrupted, since by your savor ye shall be convicted.*[82]

Comments by Irenaeus

Irenaeus suggested that "salt" represents the Church, the

---

[79] *The Spurgeon Sermon Collection*; Ages Software, Version 1, Albany, OR.; "Joseph Attacked By The Archers;" p. 187.
[80] Ibid, "Lions Lacking but the Children Satisfied," p. 393.
[81] *The Anti-Nicene Fathers, Vol 1*, "The Letter of Ignatius to the Ephesians," Ages Software, Albany, OR, Version 1.0; p. 108.
[82] *The Anti-Nicene Fathers; Vol 1*, "The Letter of Ignatius to the Magnesians," Ages Software, Albany, OR.; Version 1.0, p. 127.

99

foundation of faith.

> And while these things were taking place, his wife remained in [the territory of] Sodom, no longer corruptible flesh, but a pillar of salt which endures for ever; and by those natural processes which appertain to the human race, indicating that **the Church** also, **which is the salt of the** earth, has been left behind within the confines of the earth, and subject to human sufferings; and while entire members are often taken away from it, the pillar of salt still endures, **thus typifying the foundation of the faith** which maketh strong, and sends forward, children to their Father.[83] [my emphasis]

The Roman Catholics' Use of Salt

The Roman Catholics use salt in exorcism, apparently calling a possessed person a "creature of salt."

> **"THE EXORCISM OF THE SALT**." I exorcise thee, 0 creature of salt, in the name of the Father (†) Omnipotent, and in the love of our (†) Lord Jesus Christ, and in the virtue of the Holy (†) Spirit. I exorcise thee by the living (†) God, by the true (†) God, by the holy (†) God, who hath created thee for the safeguard of mankind, and hath commanded it to be consecrated by his servants for the people that come to believe, that in the name of the holy Trinity thou beest made a wholesome sacrament to put the enemy to flight. Therefore we pray thee, 0 our Lord God, that in sanctifying (†) thou dost sanctify this creature of salt, and in blessing (†) thou dost bless it, that it may be a perfect medicine to all that take it."[84]

---

[83] *The Anti-Nicene Fathers*, Edited by Phillip Schaff, Ages Software, Version 1.0, Albany, OR, *Irenaeus,* p. 1005.

[84] Ibid, Vol. 10, Section 4 of the Preface, p. 123-124.

Augustine's Major Premise

Many authors call Christians the salt based on "Ye are the Salt." They are too numerous to enumerate. But, it should be noted that this was Augustine's major premise for "salt" and his claim that the need for "salt" was to rid the world of the errors of "corruption."

> "the prayers of the salts who are spiritual,"[85] "God has chosen you, in order that through you He might remove the error of others?"[86]

Comments by John Chrysostom

John Chrysostom (347–407 A.D.) seemed to understand the meaning of "salt" and its application better than others at one point in his discourses. In his discussion of the charges to Timothy by Paul he relates the importance of several passages referring to the Scripture [2 Tim. 3: 15-16, 1 Tim 4: 13, Tit. 1 :9]; and then states:

> "But that the apostle gives the same charge to the laity, hear what he says in another epistle to other than the priesthood: "Let the word of Christ dwell in you richly in all wisdom," and again, "Let your speech be always with grace seasoned with salt, that ye may know how ye ought to answer each one," and there is a general charge to all that they "be ready to" render an account of their faith."[87]

Yet in other places he reverts to the priesthood of believers being the "salt."

---

[85] *The Nicene and Post Nicene Fathers Vol 4* Ages Software, Albany, OR, Version 1.0; p. 773.
[86] Ibid, Vol 6; *The Sermon on The Mount,* Book 1, p. 29.
[87] Ibid; Vol 9; *Treatise Concerning the Christian Priesthood,* Book 4, p. 117.

"Priests are the salt of the earth."[88]

Chrysostom does report that 'someone' already "spoilt," or in other words has not experienced the new birth cannot be sprinkled with "salt" because something "spoilt" is "already" decayed. Therefore no amount of sprinkling with "salt" will do any good.

> "What then? did they restore the decayed? By no means; for neither is it possible to do any good to that which is already spoilt, by sprinkling it with salt. This therefore they did not. But rather, what things had been before restored, and committed to their charge, and freed from that ill savor, these they then salted, maintaining and preserving them in that freshness, which they had received of the Lord."[89]

Lastly, Chrysostom called the Living Word "salt." Chrysostom was commenting on Judas at the last supper whose feet Jesus had just washed.

> *"And supper being ended, the devil having now put it ir,to the heart of Judas to betray Him."* This the Evangelist [John] hath said amazed, showing that Jesus washed the man who had already chosen to betray Him. This also proves his great wickedness, that not even the having shared **the salt** restrained him, (a thing which is most able to restrain wickedness;) not the fact that even up to the last day, his **Master** continued to bear with him. [my clarification my emphasis][90]

---

[88] Ibid, Vol 9, Book 6, p. 132; See also the *Homilies of St. John Chrysostom,* Vol 10, p. 184.

[89] Ibid, Vol. 14; The Homilies of St John Chrysostom on the Gospel of John, p. 220.

[90] Ibid, Vol. 14; The Homilies of St John Chrysostom on the Gospel of John, p. 575.

A Comment by Athanasius

Athanasius wrote the "beloved fellow minister" and bishop of Tyre concerning the heretics and the proper response to them.

> "And enter upon no controversy with the heretics, but overcome their argumentativeness with silence, their ill-will with courtesy. For thus your speech shall be 'with grace, seasoned with salt,' while they [will be judged] by the conscience of all."[91]

A Comment by Gregory of Nyssa

Gregory of Nyssa wrote Peter, Bishop of Sabasteia, a letter with sentiments that suggest he considered "salt" to be the words of Scripture.

> "The feeling shown in your treatise will be grateful, as salt, to the palate of the soul. As bread cannot be eaten, according to Job, without salt, so the discourse which is not savored with the inmost sentiments of God's word will never wake, and never move, desire."[92]

A Comment by Jerome

Jerome thought that the priest and bishop were "salt,"

> "And then there is the fact that the priest intercedes with God for the sinful people, while there is no one to

---

[91] The Nicene and Post-Nicene Fathers, Second Series. Vol 4: Ages Software, Version 1.0, Albany, OR; "St. Athanasius' Selected Works and Letters", The Festal Letters, 2. Personal Letters; p. 1345.
[92] Ibid, Selected Writings of Gregory, Bishop of Nyssa, Gregory of Nyssa against Eunomius, Letter 1, p. 75.

entreat for the priest. Now these two passages of Scripture tend to the same conclusion." [Mat 5:13, 1 Pe 2:9] For as salt seasons all food and nothing is so pleasant as to please the palate without it: so the bishop is the seasoning of the whole world and of his own Church, and if he lose his savor through the denial of truth, or through heresy, or lust, or, to comprehend all in one word, through sin of any kind, by what other can he be seasoned, when he was the seasoning of all?"[93] [my addition]

A Comment by Cyril, Bishop of Jerusalem

Cyril, Bishop of Jerusalem, recorded his thoughts about the meaning of "salt" according to Augustine.

"But the Bingham maintains "that: S. Augustine here refers only to the symbolical use of salt, of which he says in his *Confessions, I. xi.*, that while, yet a boy he "used to be marked with the sign of His Cross, and seasoned with His salt." The meaning of this so-called "Sacrament of the Catechumens" was that by the symbol of salt "they might learn to purge and cleanse their souls from sin."[94]

A Comment by Hilary of Poitiers

Hilary of Poitiers, greatly influenced by Origen, the perverter of Scripture and Neo-Platonist of Alexandria, records these thoughts about salt:

"A lie, he says, is often necessary, and deliberate falsehood sometimes useful. We may mislead an assassin, and so enable his intended victim to escape;

---

[93] Ibid, Vol. 6, The Principle Works of St. Jerome, "Treatises, Dialogue Against Luciferians;" p. 698.
[94] Ibid, Vol. 7, Introduction, Chapter 2, p. 30-31.

our testimony may save a defendant who is in peril in the courts; we may have to cheer a sick man by making light of his ailment. Such are the cases in which the Apostle says that our speech is to be 'seasoned with salt.'[95]

Comments by Gregory the Great
and Ephraim the Syrian

Gregory the Great undoubtedly understood the typology of "salt." Instructing pastors in proper speaking, he says:

"For on this account the Truth says, Have salt in yourselves, and have peace one with another (Mark 9:49). **Now by salt is denoted the word of wisdom**. Let him, therefore, who strives to speak wisely fear greatly, lest by his eloquence the unity of his hearers be disturbed...But the wisdom that is from above is first pure, then peaceable (James 3: 14, 15, 17). Pure, that is to say, because its ideas are chaste; and also peaceable, because it in no wise through elation disjoins itself from the society of neighbors."[96][my emphasis]

Gregory the Great repeatedly made the preceding assertions in his work. Ephraim the Syrian made similar comments.

"The prophets' sweet salt is today sprinkled among the Gentiles. Let us gain a new savor by that whereby the ancient people lost their savor. Let us speak **the speech of wisdom;** speak we not of things outside it, lest we ourselves be outside it!"... "Glory be to Him on high, Who mixed **His salt** in our minds,"... And the hundred and fifty Psalms that he wrote, in Thee were seasoned, because all **the sayings of prophecy**

---

[95] Ibid, Vol. 9, Chapter 2, *The Theology of St. Hilary of Poitiers,* p. 142.
[96] Ibid, Vol 12, *Saint Gregory the Great,* "Pastoral Rule," Chapter 4, p.503, 581, 937.

stood in need of Thy sweetness, for without **Thy salt** all manner of wisdom were tasteless.[97] [my emphasis]

Obviously these latter two men "got it!" Obviously the modern textual critics do not "get it."

A Comment by Eusebius

Salt was used to torture Christians in various stages of martyrdom. Eusebius reports the sufferings of one poor soul.

But as he was unmoved by these sufferings, and his bones were already appearing, they mixed vinegar with salt and poured it upon the mangled parts of his body.[98]

The International Bible Dictionary relates that:

"**Salt** is emblematic of **loyalty** and friendship...A person once joined in a "salt covenant" with God and then breaks it is fit only to be cast out."[99] [my emphasis, HDW]

Salt is "emblematic" of far more than "loyalty and friendship" in the Covenant of Salt and in the Scriptures. The theme of salt as "loyalty and friendship" is pervasive through much of the literature. Jesus and His words are our friends, but the typology of "salt" goes far beyond just "loyalty and friendship."

---

[97] Ibid, Vol. 13, *Hymns and Homilies of Ephraim the Syrian,* Second Part, p.423, 429, 451.
[98] *The Nicene and Post-Nicene Fathers, Second Series Vol. 1;* Ages Software, Version 1.0, Albany, OR; Book 8, p. 421.
[99] *International Standard Bible Encyclopedia*; The AGES Digital Library, Ages Software; Albany, OR, Version 10. 1997, Vol 9.

Comments by H. Clay Trumbull

H. Clay Trumbull wrote an entire book on the Covenant of Salt. He made it clear from the very beginning that the use of "salt" is not very well understood by anyone. He says:

> "The precise significance and symbolism of salt as the nexus of a lasting covenant is by no means generally understood or clearly defined by even scholars and scientists."[100]

Clay Trumbull's final conclusion is found on the cover of his 160-page book, which reflects evidence of many hours of research concerning salt.

> "Salt...symbolizes, blood and life...the supreme gift from the Supreme Giver. The Covenant of Salt, as a form or phase of the Blood Covenant, is a covenant fixed, permanent, and unchangeable, enduring forever."[101]

This comes close, but probably misses the mark. Salt represents the preserved, pure words of: Scripture, the Living Word, the Eternal Covenant, and Jesus Christ who is The Covenant and The Eternal Covenant. Trumbull's description of salt, and its use in the *secular* literature, is excellent. He points out in one place that salt has been used as an unalterable oath.

> "The Persian term for a "traitor" is **namak haram,** "untrue to salt", "one faithless to salt" and the same idea runs through the languages of the Oriental world."[102]

---

[100] Clay H. Trumbull, *The Salt Covenant*, Impact Christian Books, Inc., Kirkwood, Mo.; 1999; ISBN #0-89228-079-4); p. 11.
[101] Ibid; cover of the book.
[102] Ibid; p. 101

My sincere belief is that the interpretations of the meaning of salt by secular societies, such as the Persians, originated from the Bible, rather than the Bible's usage of salt from secular society as implied by Trumbull.[103]

Hopefully the reader now has an appreciation for the three parts of the Covenant of Salt as it pertains to the Words of God mentioned in the Preface of this work or to the Lord Jesus Christ, which are: **1. Pure, 2. Preserved, and 3. Eternal.** As such, perhaps a deeper understanding of *"the salt of the covenant of thy God"* has been achieved also.

Namak Haram: Untrue to Salt

Various authors have presented the evidence that many cultures use salt as a covenant, oath, or pledge. Has the "'modernist" and "postmodernist" committed **namak haram?** In other words, have they been "untrue to salt," when salt is defined as the pure, preserved, eternal words of God and/or as Jesus Christ? It is an expression that is still used in India to indicate a person who cannot be trusted.[104]

In conclusion, each of us must ask ourselves, "Have we been **namak haram?"** (*untrue* to salt as defined by this presentation). My sincere belief is that the apostasy of the last days is characterized by **namak haram.**

If this author may be allowed liberty, Jesus is our "Rock" of Salt. May those who claim His name stand upon the "Rock" and upon His "Salt."

---

[103] This is similar to the phenomena of the flood appearing in the stories of cultures around the world.

[104] Namak haram is used as an idiom. It means a person you can't trust because he is untrue to a covenant or promise represented by salt. Namak halal, means a very faithful person.
http://www.urbandictionary.com/define.php?term=namak

INDEX

ABOUT THE AUTHOR

Dr. Williams was born in Ft. Pierce, Florida. He was saved at the age of fourteen at his local Baptist church under Pastor J. R. White where he was active in the church youth group. His local church ordained him to preach the gospel. After graduating with honors from high school, he attended Stetson University where he met his wife, Patricia, and they were married in 1961. Starting in the ministerial program at Stetson and switching to pre-med in his junior year, he graduated with honors with a B.A. After Stetson, he taught high school at Eau Gallie, Florida for two years, and then continued his training at the University of Miami Medical School where he graduated with honors. Following his medical training, Dr. Williams and Patricia settled in New Port Richey, Florida where he practiced Family Medicine as a board certified family practitioner. He was active in his community as a hospital board member for twenty years, a chief-of-staff, president of the medical society, an advisory board member and president of Moody Bible Institute's Florida program, a board member of the Health Planning Commission, and a teacher at his local Baptist church. He helped develop and administrate a multi-specialist medical clinic with forty thousand patients and seventeen doctors. His Biblical training was obtained at Stetson University, Moody Bible Institute, and Louisiana Baptist University. After retirement, Dr. Williams has served the Lord Jesus Christ as an associate pastor, a teacher, and as vice-president and representative for the Dean Burgon Society. He received a Ph.D. in Biblical studies from Louisiana Baptist University. He has traveled to many foreign lands where he has represented the Dean Burgon Society, teaching pastors and participating in evangelistic events. He is author of the several books, *The Lie That Changed The Modern World; Word-For-Word Translating of the Received Texts, Verbal Plenary Translating; Hearing the Voice of God; The*

Septuagint is a Paraphrase; The Pure Words of God; The Attack on the Canon of Scripture; The Miracle of Biblical Inspiration; Origin of the Critical Text; The Covenant of Salt; and *Wycliffe Controversies,* in addition to many articles and booklets. He is President of "The Old Paths Publications," which helps authors publish their works by the modern method of printing on demand (POD) and a board member of "The William Carey Bible Society." Dr. Williams' Bible studies can currently be seen by archived or live streaming through Bible For Today ministries. Dr. Williams and his wife, Patricia have two sons, five grandchildren, and two great-grandchildren.

BOOKS BY DR. WILLIAMS

HEARING THE VOICE OF GOD:

This 264 page perfect bound book was released in January, 2008. ISBN 978-0-9801689-0-7. You may purchase it at Amazon.com. or at BibleForToday.org, BFT # **3340**.

Dr. Williams' book, *Hearing the Voice of God,* discusses the critical factors related to the postmodern confusion surrounding this issue. He approaches the subject clearly and realistically from a biblicist's point of view. Mysticism is refuted. Individuals desiring the truth about God speaking to them will appreciate this volume. Many present day teachers cause emotionally distressed people to turn to their own thoughts, as if their thoughts were God speaking to them. This work investigates the topic as it relates to revelation, conscience, inspiration, illumination, and the voice of the Lord in Scripture. Dr. Williams explains how postmodern philosophy has created an atmosphere that contributes to the confusion surrounding this important subject.

www.theoldpathspublications.com, www.biblefortoday.org.

WORD-FOR-WORD TRANSLATING OF THE RECEIVED TEXT, VERBAL PLENARY TRANSLATING:

This 264 page perfect bound book may be purchased on Amazon or www.BibleForToday.org. See below. There is a vital need for a book to inform sincere Bible-believing Christians about the proper techniques of translating the WORDS of God into the receptor languages of the world. No book like this one has ever been written. It is a unique and much-needed book. The very first requirement for any translation of the Bible is to have the proper WORDS of Hebrew, Aramaic, and Greek from which to translate. It is the contention of this book that the original verbally and plenarily inspired Hebrew, Aramaic, and Greek WORDS have been verbally and plenarily preserved in accordance with God's promises. These preserved WORDS are those received-text-WORDS which underlie the King James Bible. This volume emphasizes the requirement of a proper technique to be used in all translations of God's WORDS. It must be done in a verbally and plenarily translation technique. That is, the Hebrew, Aramaic, and Greek WORDS must be conveyed into the receptor languages, not merely the ideas, concepts, thoughts, or message. This technique is absent in all of the other manuals on Bible translation. Dr. Williams is not the usual sort of writer. He combines the meticulous skill of a Doctor of Medicine with the artistry and acumen of a Doctor of

Philosophy to produce this grand volume. May translators and sincere Christians of all persuasions and professions use this important book worldwide! The Bible For Today Press, BFT #**3302** ISBN 1-56848-056-3, Order by PHONE: 1-800-JOHN 10:9, Order by FAX: 856-854-2464, Order by MAIL: Bible For Today, 900 Park Avenue Collingswood, NJ 08108"

THE ATTACK ON THE CANON OF SCRIPTURE, A POLEMIC AGAINST MODERN SCHOLARSHIP

This 264 page perfect bound book was released in January, 2008. ISBN 978-0-9801689-0-7. This 152 page book demonstrates the newest attack on the Words and books of the Bible by modern day scholarship. The changing methods for assaulting the Scriptures are important for those who are concerned about the relentless attempt to destroy them. In a remarkable polemic against modern scholarship, Dr. Williams outlines the most recent means many are using to undermine confidence in the Words of God received through the priesthood of believers. It is available at Amazon.com. or at BibleForToday.org, BFT # **3340**.

THE LIE THAT CHANGED THE MODERN WORLD

This book is perfect bound, 440 pages in all. ISBN 1-56848-042-3. It is a factual defense not only of the King James Bible, but also of the Hebrew and Greek Words that underlie the King James Bible. The author is a medical doctor, now retired, who has researched this important topic thoroughly. May the Lord Jesus Christ use and honor this study in the days, weeks, months, and years ahead until our Lord Jesus Christ returns. It should be in every layman's library, every Pastor's library, every church library, every college library, every university library, and in every theological seminary library. It is available at Amazon or through Bible For Today Press, www.biblefortoday.org, BFT # **3125**.

THE PURE WORDS OF GOD

This is a perfect bound 136 page book. ISBN 978-0-9801689-1-4. Dr. Williams' book, *The Pure Words of God,* clarifies the use of the word "pure" when it is used to define the Words of God. Should "pure" be applied to translations, to Traditional/Received Texts, or to critical texts? Once the correct application is explained, Dr. Williams clarifies God's commands to receive and keep His pure Words. It is available through Amazon.com or Bible For Today Press at:

www.biblefortoday.org, BFT #3344

THE MIRACLE OF BIBLICAL INSPIRATION

The book is a 130 page perfect bound book. ISBN 978-0-9820608-6-5. There are numerous opinions in the literature concerning the meaning of "inspiration" of the Bible such as "the partial view," "the natural view," "the neoorthodox view," "the pagan view," and many others. The explanation of most of the various views is very troubling. Very few positions exalt the true origin of the original Words of the Bible in Hebrew, Aramaic, and Greek. The positions fail to correctly recognize that the process and the product of "inspiration" is a **miracle** *"once delivered."* Dr. Williams' work will help others to understand the meaning of the words associated with "inspiration" in their Biblical context. The book is available on Amazon and may be ordered from www.BibleForToday.org., BFT#3392

THE ORIGIN OF THE CRITICAL TEXT

This is a 157 page perfect bound book. ISBN 978-0-9820608-4-1. There are five significant pivotal points pertaining to the origin of the corrupted Critical Texts that lie behind the modern versions of the Bible. It is important for believers to understand the origin and the influence of these original language texts on doctrine, practice, application, and translation of these false texts. At least one new English version of the Bible has appeared in the market place every six months for the last several decades that is translated from these texts. The five pivotal points associated with six men are:

Satan: The initiator of the devious disrespect for and changing of the Words of God began with that old serpent the Devil "in the beginning" (Gen. 3, and Mat. 4).

Origen: The first two centuries after the completion of the New Testament were the most destructive era for the Words of God. This was particularly true in Alexandria, Egypt where dozens of cults existed. Origen (182-251 AD) lived and taught in an Alexandrian theological school. He was supported by a wealthy man, Ambrosius, which allowed him to travel to many regions with an entourage of at least seven to fourteen scribes skilled in calligraphy, copying, and stenography. Wherever he went, he changed Biblical manuscripts to fit his doctrine and philosophy.

Jerome: Jerome's publication of the Latin Vulgate in 405 AD constructed from Alexandrian text-type manuscripts was a crucial key in the continued assault on the Bible. Its influence because of the Roman Catholic Church would be immense.

Darwin: The publication of Charles Darwin's book, The Origin of Species, in 1857 caused many 'scholars' to believe that the book of Genesis was a fable or myth, which destroyed confidence in the inspired Words of God.

Westcott and Hort: Westcott and Hort were two professors at Cambridge in the mid to late eighteen hundreds. One was a bishop in the Anglican Church. They constructed a 'new' false Greek text from their false tenets of textual criticism. The 'new' text would become the corrupted text behind modern versions of the Bible.

This book is available on Amazon and at www.BibleForToday.org. BFT #3386.

WYCLIFFE CONTROVERSIES

The book is 311 pages and perfect bound. ISBN 978-0-9817339-8-2. This book by Dr. Williams discusses Dr. John de Wycliffe and the controversies surrounding him and the Wycliffe Bibles such as which texts were used to translate the Bibles, who were his associates and friends and did they do the translating or assist him, who were the Lollards, and many other debates.

This book is available on Amazon and at www.BibleForToday.org. BFT #3363.

www.ingramcontent.com/pod-product-compliance
Lightning Source LLC
LaVergne TN
LVHW021358080426
835508LV00020B/2343